Contents

Back to School . . . . A

Theme 1 **Off to Adventure!**

Selection Connections 1

The Lost and Found 3

Reading-Writing Workshop:
    A Personal Narrative 18

The Ballad of Mulan 23

The Waterfall 38

Taking Tests 53

Spelling Review 55

Theme 2 **Celebrating Traditions**

Selection Connections 59

The Keeping Quilt 61

Reading-Writing Workshop:
    Instructions 76

Anthony Reynoso: Born to Rope 81

The Talking Cloth 96

Dancing Rainbows 111

Taking Tests 127

Spelling Review 129

Focus on Trickster Tales 133

i

Contents

Theme 3   **Incredible Stories**

Selection Connections 135

Dogzilla 137

Reading-Writing Workshop:
  A Story 152

The Mysterious Giant of Barletta 157

Raising Dragons 172

The Garden of Abdul Gasazi 187

Taking Tests 203

Spelling Review 205

Student Handbook 209

Spelling 211

  How to Study a Word

  Words Often Misspelled

  Take-Home Word Lists

Grammar and Usage: Problem Words . . 225

Proofreading Checklist 226

Proofreading Marks 227

Name _____

Strategy Workshop

As you listen to the story "The Rule," by Anne Cameron, you will stop from time to time to do some activities on these practice pages. These activities will help you think about different strategies that can help you read better. After completing each activity, you will discuss what you've written with your classmates and talk about how to use these strategies.

Remember, strategies can help you become a better reader. Good readers

- use strategies whenever they read

- use different strategies before, during, and after reading

- think about how strategies will help them

Name _____

Strategy 1: Predict/Infer

Use this strategy before and during reading to help make
predictions about what happens next or what you're going
to learn.

Here's how to use the Predict/Infer strategy:

1. Think about the title, the illustrations, and what you
   have read so far.
2. Tell what you think will happen next—or what you will
   learn. Thinking about what you already know about
   the subject may help.
3. Try to figure out things the author does not say
   directly.

Listen as your teacher begins "The Rule." When your teacher
stops, complete the activity with a partner to show that you
understand how to predict what you think might happen in the
story.

Think about the story and respond to the question below.

What do you think might happen in the story?

_____

_____

As you continue listening to the story, think about whether
your prediction was right. You might want to change your
prediction or write a new one below.

_____

_____

_____

Name _____

Strategy 2: Phonics/Decoding

Use this strategy during reading when you come across a
word you don't know.

Here's how to use the Phonics/Decoding strategy:

    1. Look carefully at the word.

    2. Look for word parts that you know and think about
       the sounds for the letters.

    3. Blend the sounds to read the word.

    4. Ask yourself if this is a word you know and whether
       the word makes sense in the sentence.

    5. If not, ask yourself if there is anything else you could
       try—should you look in the dictionary?

Listen as your teacher continues to read the story. When your
teacher stops, use the Phonics/Decoding strategy.

Now write down the steps you used to decode the word *trout*.

_____

_____

_____

_____

_____

_____

Remember to use this strategy whenever you are reading and
come across a word that you don't know.

Name _____

Strategy 3: Monitor/Clarify

Use this strategy during reading whenever you're confused about what you are reading.

Here's how to use the Monitor/Clarify strategy:

- Ask yourself if what you're reading makes sense—or if you are learning what you need to learn.
- If you don't understand something, reread, look at the illustrations, or read ahead to see if that helps.

Listen as your teacher continues to read the story. When your teacher stops, complete the activity with a partner to show that you understand how to figure out why the boy in the story might think the mushrooms look like a forest.

Think about the story and respond below.

1. Have you ever eaten mushrooms? What do they look like?

   _____

   _____

2. Can you tell from listening to the story why the boy may have thought the mushrooms looked like a forest? Why or why not?

   _____

   _____

3. How can you find out why he may have thought that?

   _____

   _____

Name _____

Strategy 4: Question

Use this strategy during and after reading to ask questions about important ideas in the story.

Here's how to use the Question strategy:

- Ask yourself questions about important ideas in the story.
- Ask yourself if you can answer these questions.
- If you can't answer the questions, reread and look for answers in the text. Thinking about what you already know and what you've read in the story may help you.

Listen as your teacher continues to read the story. Then complete the activity with a partner to show that you understand how to ask yourself questions about important ideas in the story.

Think about the story and respond below.

Write a question you might ask yourself at this point in the story.

_____

_____

_____

_____

_____

If you can't answer your question now, think about it while you listen to the rest of the story.

Name _____

Strategy 5: Evaluate

Use this strategy during and after reading to help you form an opinion about what you read.

Here's how to use the Evaluate strategy:

- Think about how the author makes the story come alive and makes you want to read it.
- Think about what was entertaining, informative, or useful about the selection.
- Think about how you reacted to the story—how well you understood the selection and whether you enjoyed reading it.

Listen as your teacher continues to read the story. When your teacher stops, complete the activity with a partner to show that you are thinking of how you feel about what you are reading and why you feel that way.

Think about the story and respond below.

1. Tell whether or not you think this story is entertaining and why.

_____

_____

2. This is a humorous, realistic fiction story. Did the author make the characters interesting and believable?

_____

_____

3. How did you react to this story?

_____

Name _____

Strategy 6: Summarize

Use this strategy after reading to summarize what you read.

Here's how to use the Summarize strategy:
- Think about the characters.
- Think about where the story takes place.
- Think about the problem in the story and how the characters solve it.
- Think about what happens in the beginning, middle, and end of the story.

Think about the story you just listened to. Complete the activity with a partner to show that you understand how to identify important story parts that will help you summarize the story.

Think about the story and respond to the questions below:

1. Who is the main character?

_____

_____

2. Where does the story take place?

_____

_____

3. What is the problem and how is it resolved?

_____

_____

Now use this information to summarize the story for a partner.

Name _____

Strategy: Summarize

Use this strategy after reading to summarize what you read.

Here's how to use the Summarize strategy.
- Think about the characters.
- Think about where the story takes place.
- Think about the problem in the story and how the characters solve it.
- Think about what happens in the beginning, middle, and end of the story.

Think about the story you just listened to. Complete the activity with a partner to show that you understand how to identify important story parts that will help you summarize the story.

Think about the story and respond to the questions below.

1. Who is the main character?

_____

_____

2. Where does the story take place?

_____

_____

3. What is the problem and how is it resolved?

_____

_____

Now use this information to summarize the story for a partner.

Name _____

Off to Adventure!

Cut out a picture of something you think is an adventure from a magazine or a newspaper. Paste it on this page. Then answer the questions below. Answers will vary.

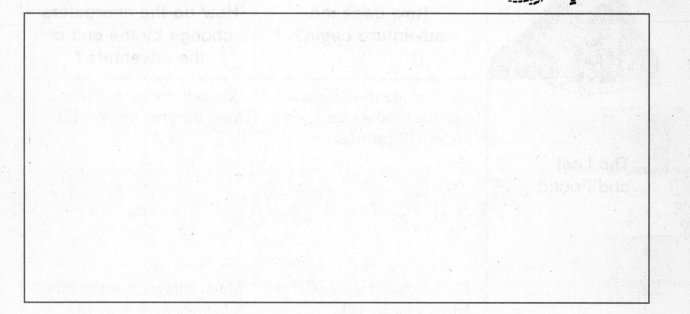

1. What do you think makes this an adventure?

   (3 points) _____

   _____

2. How would you describe this adventure to someone?

   (3) _____

   _____

3. Would you like to be part of this adventure? Explain your answer.

   (4) _____

   _____

Name _____

Off to Adventure!

As you read each selection in *Off to Adventure!*, fill in the boxes of the chart that apply to the selection. Sample answers shown.
(5 points per selection)

	How does the adventure begin?	How do the characters change by the end of the adventure?
The Lost and Found	Three students disappear into the school's Lost and Found. **(2 points)**	Wendell, Floyd, and Mona have become friends. **(3)**
The Ballad of Mulan	Mulan joins the army in her father's place. **(2)**	Mulan shows courage and becomes a general. **(3)**
The Waterfall	A family hikes until they come to a waterfall. **(2)**	The family finds out that it is possible to climb the waterfall. **(3)**

Assessment Tip: Total **15** Points

Name _____

What a Day!

Joey has just moved to a new town. Help him finish a letter to his friend. Fill in the blanks with the correct words from the box.

Vocabulary

rumpled
situations
worried
visible
unusual
directions

September 5

Dear Flora:

My first day of school was full of unlucky

<u>situations</u> **(2 points)**_____. I wanted to wear my favorite

shirt, but it was all <u>rumpled</u> **(2)**_____ from being

packed in a box. While I was looking for something else to

wear, I missed the bus. My parents drove me to school, but we

got lost on the way. We had to stop and ask for

<u>directions</u> **(2)**_____. I was <u>worried</u> **(2)**_____

that I would be late for school, but we got there just in time.

At noon, I couldn't find my lunchbox. I looked everywhere,

but it wasn't <u>visible</u> **(2)**_____. Then my day got

better. Some nice students asked me to sit with them. They

shared their lunches with me. It was an <u>unusual</u> **(2)**_____ way

to make new friends, but I'm glad it happened!

Your friend,

Joey

Name _____

Event Map

Pages 20–21

Wendell and Floyd are at the principal's office. Then Mona

enters and says she wants to look in the Lost and Found for her

lucky hat. **(2 points)**

Page 23

Mona leans so far into the bin that only her feet are showing.

A moment later, she disappears. **(2)**

Pages 26–27

The boys climb into the Lost and Found bin to find Mona. **(2)**

Pages 30–31

The children see a sign to the Hat Room, so they follow a

passageway to a cave, a lake, a suit of armor, and a boat. **(2)**

Pages 34–37

The children come to a hallway lined with doors. Finally, Mona opens

one last door and finds the Hat Room. **(2)**

4   Theme 1: **Off to Adventure!**
Assessment Tip: Total **10** Points

Name _____

Tell the True Story

**The underlined part of each sentence below is false.
Rewrite it as a true sentence about *The Lost and Found*.**

1. Wendell and Floyd are waiting to see the principal because they missed <u>their bus</u>.

    Wendell and Floyd are waiting to see the principal because they

    missed a math test. **(2 points)**

2. Mona walks into the office to <u>borrow some lunch money</u>.

    Mona walks into the office to look for her lucky hat in the Lost

    and Found bin. **(2)**

3. The boys want to climb into the Lost and Found bin to <u>get away from a giant squid</u>.

    The boys want to climb into the Lost and Found bin to find

    Mona. **(2)**

4. The children cross the lake to find <u>the school library</u>.

    The children cross the lake to find the Hat Room and Mona's

    lucky hat. **(2)**

5. In the Hat Room, the boys start <u>looking for their lost baseball caps</u>.

    In the Hat Room, the boys start trying on hats to find lucky

    ones of their own. **(2)**

6. Mona finds her lucky hat <u>hanging on the Hat Room door</u>.

    Mona finds her lucky hat in her purse. **(2)**

Name _____

Story Events

Read the story. Think about what happens. Then fill in the chart on the next page.

Surprise!

After a long drive, Mom, Dad, and I got to Golden Lake. We were tired, so we set up camp and climbed into our sleeping bags. Then I said, "I hate camping. Why did you make me come?"

"You never know what can happen, Jenny," Dad answered. "You could be in for a big surprise!"

The next morning, I couldn't believe my eyes. There, sitting by the tent was a bee the size of an airplane! "Hop on!" shouted Dad over its loud hum. "Come for a ride."

We all got onto the bee's big, fuzzy back. Then it lifted off. It zoomed right and left. It sailed over the water and made loops in the air. What a fun ride!

At last, the bee landed by our camp. We all climbed off. Then it flew away. I stood there with my mouth open. Dad smiled and said, "Just wait until tomorrow's surprise!"

Name _____

Story Events continued

Fill in the blanks to tell what happened in the story.

The family sets up camp at Golden Lake.

↓

Jenny says she hates camping, but Dad tells her she may be in for a surprise.

↓

The next morning Jenny sees a bee as big as a plane. **(2)**

↓

The family climbs onto its back.

↓

Then the bee takes the family for a ride. **(2)**

↓

At last the bee lands back at the campsite. **(2)**

↓

The family climbs off.

↓

The bee flies away. **(2)**

Name _____

Base Words

Some words are formed from a **base word,** a word that can stand by itself. In the word *climbing*, the base word is *climb*. Letters can be added to the beginning or the end of a base word, as you see here.

appear/**dis**appear   boat/boat**er**   turn/turn**ed**

Some of the words in this Lost and Found bin contain base words. Circle the base word in those words. Then write each base word on the lines below.

asked   unusual   closer   only
principal   trying   nonsense   loosely

1._____ ask _____

2._____ usual _____

3._____ try _____

4._____ close _____

5._____ sense _____

6._____ loose _____

Assessment Tip: Total **6** Points

Name _____

Short Vowels

► A short vowel sound is usually spelled with one vowel followed by a consonant sound.

The /ă/ sound is usually spelled **a,** as in l**a**st.
The /ĕ/ sound is usually spelled **e,** as in sm**e**ll.
The /ĭ/ sound is usually spelled **i,** as in m**i**x.

► Sometimes the /ĕ/ sound is spelled in a different way. In the starred words *head* and *friend*, the /ĕ/ sound is spelled *ea* and *ie*.

Write each Spelling Word under its vowel sound.
Order of answers for each category may vary.

Spelling Words

1. mix
2. milk
3. smell
4. last
5. head*
6. friend*
7. class
8. left
9. thick
10. send
11. thin
12. stick

/ă/ Sound

last **(1 point)**

class **(1)**

/ĭ/ Sound

mix **(1)**

milk **(1)**

thick **(1)**

thin **(1)**

stick **(1)**

/ĕ/ Sound

smell **(1)**

head **(1)**

friend **(1)**

left **(1)**

send **(1)**

Theme 1: **Off to Adventure!**   9
Assessment Tip: Total **12** Points

Name _____

Spelling Spree

Silly Rhymes Write a Spelling Word to complete each silly sentence. Each answer rhymes with the underlined word.

1. Will chewing gum _____ to a <u>brick</u>?
2. Don't pile <u>bread</u> on your _____!
3. Never drink _____ while wearing <u>silk</u>.
4. You have to be _____ to squeeze under a <u>bin</u>.
5. <u>Fix</u> the ladder and _____ the batter.
6. How can you <u>tell</u> if bees can _____?

Spelling Words
1. mix
2. milk
3. smell
4. last
5. head*
6. friend*
7. class
8. left
9. thick
10. send
11. thin
12. stick

1. <u>stick **(1 point)**</u>   4. <u>thin **(1)**</u>

2. <u>head **(1)**</u>   5. <u>mix **(1)**</u>

3. <u>milk **(1)**</u>   6. <u>smell **(1)**</u>

Letter Math Write a Spelling Word by adding and taking away letters from the words below.

Example: d + fish - f = *dish*

7. spend - p   = <u>send **(1)**</u>

8. c + glass - g   = <u>class **(1)**</u>

9. leg - g + ft   = <u>left **(1)**</u>

10. fri + mend - m   = <u>friend **(1)**</u>

11. blast - b   = <u>last **(1)**</u>

12. th + sick - s   = <u>thick **(1)**</u>

Assessment Tip: Total **12** Points

Name _____

Proofreading and Writing

Proofreading Circle the five misspelled Spelling Words in the sign. Then write each word correctly.

MY HAT IS LOST!

Please help me find my hat. I don't know where I (leaft) it. The hat is green and has a (thine) blue ribbon. It is soft and kind of rumpled. The last time I had it was before (clas) on Monday. If you find it, please (stik) a note on my locker.

A (freind) and classmate

Spelling Words

1. mix
2. milk
3. smell
4. last
5. head*
6. friend*
7. class
8. left
9. thick
10. send
11. thin
12. stick

1. left **(2 points)** _____

2. thin **(2)** _____

3. class **(2)** _____

4. stick **(2)** _____

5. friend **(2)** _____

Write a Description Have you ever lost something that you liked very much, such as a piece of clothing or a toy?

On a separate sheet of paper, write a short description of the item you lost. Make sure to include details that would help someone recognize it. Use Spelling Words from the list. (2)

Responses will vary.

Name _____

Find the Right Order

The words in the Lost Bin have simply been tossed in any old order. Put the words in alphabetical order and write them in the Found Bin.

LOST BIN

muddle	principal
paddle	suggest
squeeze	crazy
plunge	mutter
middle	groan

FOUND BIN

1. crazy **(1 point)**
2. groan **(1)**
3. middle **(1)**
4. muddle **(1)**
5. mutter **(1)**

6. paddle **(1)**
7. plunge **(1)**
8. principal **(1)**
9. squeeze **(1)**
10. suggest **(1)**

12   Theme 1: **Off to Adventure!**
Assessment Tip: Total **10** Points

Name _____

Finding Sentences

Read each group of words. Write *sentence* if the words are a complete sentence. Write *fragment* if the words are not a complete sentence. Then rewrite each fragment as a complete sentence. Add a word or words from the box at the bottom of the page.

Sentences for completed fragments will vary. Suggested sentences given.

1. Floyd wanted a hat. _sentence_ **(2 points)**

   _____

2. Examined a suit of armor. _fragment_ **(2)**

   Wendell examined a suit of armor.

3. The rumpled lucky hat. _fragment_ **(2)**

   The rumpled lucky hat disappeared.

4. Mona looked for her missing hat. _sentence_ **(2)**

   _____

5. Floated on the water. _fragment_ **(2)**

   The boat floated on the water.

6. Flipped a coin. _fragment_ **(2)**

   Floyd flipped a coin.

Word Bank

adventures	disappeared	Floyd
Mona	the boat	Wendell
worked		

Assessment Tip: Total **12** Points

Name _____

Changing Fragments to Sentences

Use each fragment below in a complete sentence.
Answers will vary. Suggested sentences given.

1. Floyd and his friend Wendell

   Floyd and his friend Wendell fought a giant squid. **(2 points)**

2. into a lost and found box

   Three friends dive into a lost and found box. **(2)**

3. loses her lucky hat

   Mona loses her lucky hat. **(2)**

4. looks like a dragon

   The boat looks like a dragon. **(2)**

5. in the hat room

   Floyd searches in the hat room. **(2)**

6. an exciting adventure in a strange world

   They go on an exciting adventure in a strange world. **(2)**

7. decides which cave to explore

   Wendell decides which cave to explore. **(2)**

8. a burgundy fez with a small gold tassel

   Wendell wears a burgundy fez with a small gold tassel. **(2)**

Assessment Tip: Total **16** Points

Name _____

Finding Sentences

Effective writers use complete sentences. Correct each sentence fragment. Write your revised sentence on each line. If it is a complete sentence, write the word *correct*.

Lucky Hats for Lucky Cats

1. Mona's cat. Likes Mona's lucky hat.

   Mona's cat likes Mona's lucky hat. **(2 points)**

2. Laughs at the ridiculous cat.

   Mona laughs at the ridiculous cat. **(2)**

3. The playful cat. Bites the floppy hat.

   The playful cat bites the floppy hat. **(2)**

4. Then the cat runs away with the hat.

   correct **(2)**

5. Chases her cat into the basement.

   Mona chases her cat into the basement. **(2)**

6. She hears. A meow.

   She hears a meow. **(2)**

7. Mona opens the suitcase.

   correct **(2)**

8. The cat. Is on her lucky hat.

   The cat is on her lucky hat. **(2)**

Assessment Tip: Total **16** Points

Name _____

Writing a Friendly Letter

The person I will write to: **(1 point)** _____

My address: **(1)** _____

_____

The date: **(1)** _____

How I will greet the receiver: **(1)** _____

Why I want to write: **(1)** _____

_____

The most important thing I want to say: **(1)** _____

_____

_____

Important details I want to include: **(1)** _____

_____

_____

How I will close: **(1)** _____

_____

Assessment Tip: Total **8** Points

Name _____

Using Commas in Dates and Places

► When writing dates, use a comma between the day and the year. **Example:** May 12, 2003

► Use a comma after the year except at the end of a sentence.

Example: On June 30, 2003, my sister will be ten years old.

► Use a comma between a town or city and the state.

Example: New Orleans, Louisiana

► Use a comma after the state except at the end of a sentence.

Example: My brother goes to college in New Orleans, Louisiana, and we will visit him next month.

Proofread the letter and add commas where necessary.

653 Cauterskill Road
(2 points) Catskills, New York, 12414
(1) February 25, 2005

Dear Uncle Frank,

Our class is taking a field trip to New York City. Mom and Dad are going to be parent helpers. We want to spend an evening with you. We take a bus to New York, **(1)** New York, on May 12, 2005, and return on the morning of **(3)** May 14, 2005. Can you let us know right away which date **(1)** is best for you?

Your nephew,
Michael

Name _____

Revising Your Personal Narrative

Reread your story. What do you need to make it better? Use this page to help you decide. Put a checkmark in the box for each sentence that describes your personal narrative.

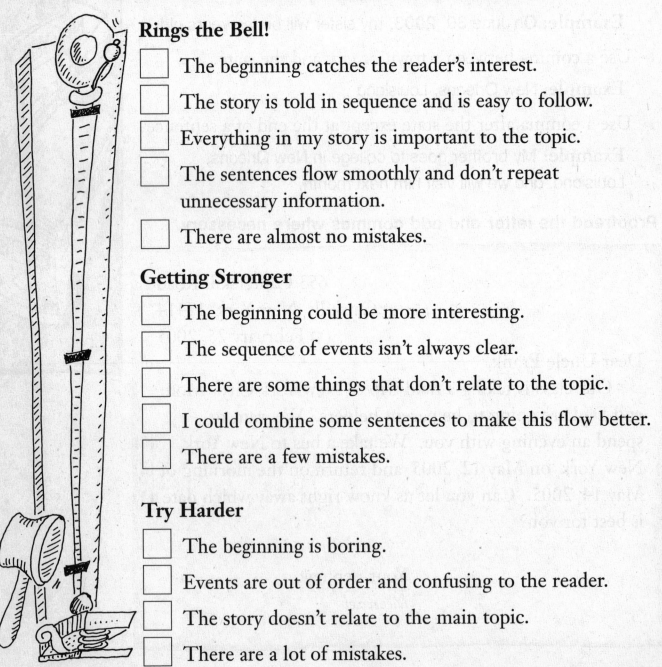

Rings the Bell!

☐ The beginning catches the reader's interest.

☐ The story is told in sequence and is easy to follow.

☐ Everything in my story is important to the topic.

☐ The sentences flow smoothly and don't repeat unnecessary information.

☐ There are almost no mistakes.

Getting Stronger

☐ The beginning could be more interesting.

☐ The sequence of events isn't always clear.

☐ There are some things that don't relate to the topic.

☐ I could combine some sentences to make this flow better.

☐ There are a few mistakes.

Try Harder

☐ The beginning is boring.

☐ Events are out of order and confusing to the reader.

☐ The story doesn't relate to the main topic.

☐ There are a lot of mistakes.

18   Theme 1: **Off to Adventure!**

Name _____

Combining Sentences

Combine each pair of sentences into one. Include all the important parts of both sentences. Avoid repeating words.

1. The water was cold. The water was full of sharks.

   The water was cold and full of sharks. **(2 points)**

   _____

2. Nina dove in the water. Brenda dove in the water.

   Nina and Brenda dove in the water. **(2)**

   _____

3. Paul screamed. Winston screamed.

   Paul and Winston screamed. **(2)**

4. Nina laughed. Nina shouted, "Come on in, fellas!"

   Nina laughed and shouted, "Come on in, fellas!" **(2)**

   _____

5. Paul said, "No way!" Winston said, "No way!"

   Paul and Winston said, "No way!" **(2)**

   _____

6. Brenda yelled, "These sharks are only toys!" Tina yelled, "These sharks are only toys!"

   Brenda and Tina yelled, "These sharks are only toys!" **(2)**

   _____

Name _____

Spelling Words

Look for spelling patterns you have learned to help you remember the Spelling Words on this page. Think about the parts that you find hard to spell.

Write the missing letters and apostrophe in the Spelling Words below.   Order of answers for 6 and 7 may vary.

Spelling Words

1. have
2. haven't
3. found
4. around
5. one
6. than
7. then
8. them
9. before
10. because
11. other
12. mother

1. hav e ____ **(1 point)**

2. hav e ____ n ____ ' ____ t ____ **(1)**

3. f o ____ u ____ nd **(1)**

4. ar o ____ u ____ nd **(1)**

5. o ____ ne **(1)**

6. th a ____ n **(1)**

7. th e ____ n **(1)**

8. th e ____ m **(1)**

9. befo r ____ e ____ **(1)**

10. bec a ____ u ____ s ____ e **(1)**

11. o ____ ther **(1)**

12. m ____ o ____ ther **(1)**

Study List On another sheet of paper, write each Spelling Word. Check the list to be sure you spell each word correctly. Order of words may vary. **(2)**

Assessment Tip: Total **14** Points

Name _____

Spelling Spree

Sentence Fillers Write the Spelling Word from the
list on this page that best completes each sentence.

Spelling Words

1–2. "Scott, _____ you seen my coat?"

    "No, I _____."

3. We drove _____ the block three times.

4. Our neighbors asked us to lend _____ our
lawnmower.

5. For a while it was noisy, but _____ it got quiet.

6. We met at the theater _____ the movie started.

7. I don't want this one, I want the _____ one.

8. Tania _____ a five-dollar bill lying on the ground.

Spelling Words

1. have
2. haven't
3. found
4. around
5. one
6. than
7. then
8. them
9. before
10. because
11. other
12. mother

1. have **(1 point)**

2. haven't **(1)**

3. around **(1)**

4. them **(1)**

5. then **(1)**

6. before **(1)**

7. other **(1)**

8. found **(1)**

Word Clues Write the Spelling Word that fits each clue best.

9. You can use this word when you give a reason.

10. This word isn't a father, but a _____.

11. This word is the first thing you say when you count.

12. You can use this word when you compare two things.

9. because **(1)**

10. mother **(1)**

11. one **(1)**

12. than **(1)**

Assessment Tip: Total **12** Points

Name _____

Proofreading and Writing

Proofreading Circle the four misspelled Spelling Words in this postcard. Then write each word correctly on the lines below.

Dear Peter,

I just wanted to send a card to say hi (befor) I get going again. I (fond) this one in a little store in Yellowknife. Things are going great, and I'll have a lot of stories to tell when I get home. I'm sorry I (havn't) written in so long. I'll try to be better about it than I have been. Say hi to Mom and Dad, and tell (then) I'll call soon.

Love,
Kim

1. before **(2 points)**

2. found **(2)**

3. haven't **(2)**

4. them **(2)**

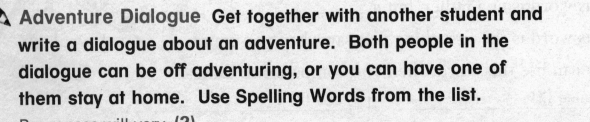

Adventure Dialogue Get together with another student and write a dialogue about an adventure. Both people in the dialogue can be off adventuring, or you can have one of them stay at home. Use Spelling Words from the list.

Responses will vary. **(2)**

Assessment Tip: Total **10** Points

Name _____

Crossword Challenge!

Write the word that matches each clue in the puzzle.
Use the words in the box and your glossary for help.

Vocabulary

| armor | comrades | endured | farewell |
| triumphant | troops | victorious | |

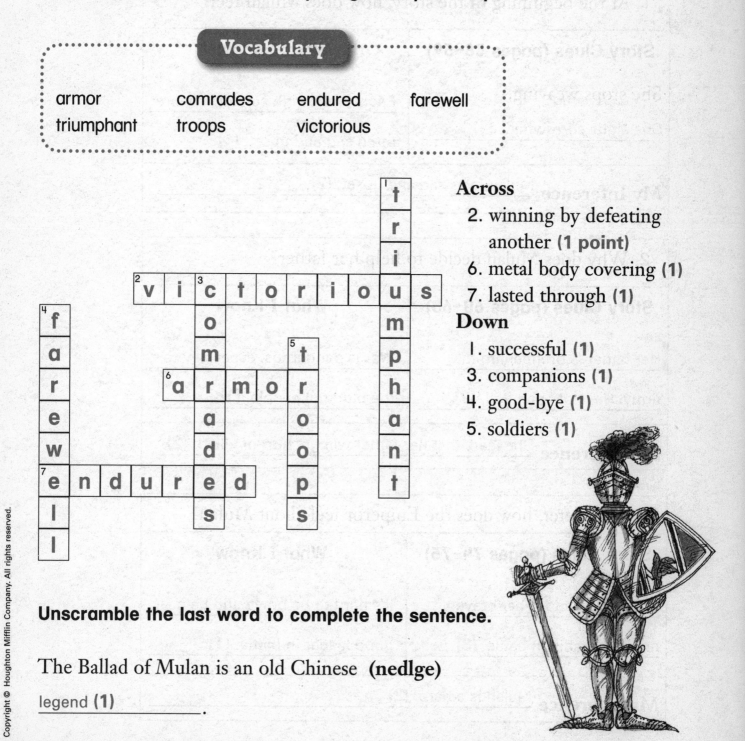

Across
2. winning by defeating another **(1 point)**
6. metal body covering **(1)**
7. lasted through **(1)**

Down
1. successful **(1)**
3. companions **(1)**
4. good-bye **(1)**
5. soldiers **(1)**

Unscramble the last word to complete the sentence.

The Ballad of Mulan is an old Chinese **(nedlge)**

legend **(1)** _____.

Name _____

Inference Chart

Responses will vary.

---

1. At the beginning of the story, how does Mulan feel?

Story Clues (pages 58–59)	**What I Know**
She stops weaving. She sighs sorrowfully. **(1)**	People who sigh sorrowfully are often sad and upset. **(1)**

My Inference Mulan feels sad and upset. **(2)**

---

2. Why does Mulan decide to help her father?

Story Clues (pages 60–63)	**What I Know**
Her father is drafted into the army. He is old and frail. **(2)**	War is dangerous, especially to the old, frail people. **(1)**

My Inference She fears that her father will get hurt or killed. **(2)**

---

3. Years later, how does the Emperor feel about Mulan?

Story Clues (pages 74–75)	**What I Know**
She is praised for her bravery and leadership in battle. **(3)**	It's hard to be brave and be a good leader in battle. **(1)**

My Inference Mulan is a hero. **(2)**

---

24   Theme 1: **Off to Adventure!**
Assessment Tip: Total **15 Points**

Name _____

Answers About Mulan

Answer these questions about *The Ballad of Mulan*.

1. Why does the Emperor need troops?

   An enemy army is attacking China. **(2 points)**

   _____

2. Why does Mulan go to war in her father's place?

   She has no older brother; her father is old and frail. **(2)**

   _____

3. After the war, why does the Emperor want to honor Mulan?

   Her skill, bravery, and leadership have helped to win battles. **(2)**

   _____

4. How does Mulan's family feel about having her come home?

   They are excited and proud; the parents come out to welcome her; her sister

   beautifies herself; her brother helps to prepare a feast. **(2)**

5. When Mulan returns home, what does she choose to do?

   She changes from her armor into a favorite dress. **(2)**

   _____

6. What is the meaning of Mulan's statement about the rabbits?

   Accept reasonable responses. Example: In times of danger, how you act is

   more important than whether you are a man or woman. **(2)**

7. Why do the Chinese still honor Mulan?

   Accept reasonable responses. Example: She showed love and respect

   for her family and country without asking for a reward. **(3)**

Name _____

Make a Good Guess

Read the story below. Then answer the questions on the following page.

The Ice Girl

Trolls were raiding the valley. They swooped down from icy mountain caves, looking for workers and burning houses and barns. Those unlucky enough to be caught never saw daylight again. The people in the valley called a meeting to deal with the problem.

Greta sat and knitted. Ever since Father had fallen, Brother was doing all the family chores. Even at this late hour, he had gone to town while Father slept. Greta helped as best she could. In her spare time, she knitted and knitted. Perhaps her work would help to keep them from selling a cow.

Suddenly, Greta heard a noise outside. Trolls! She slipped out a side door and stood waiting. Sure enough, four ugly trolls peered around the barn. Greta stood still. Slowly the trolls crept closer and closer, but Greta never moved. Finally she felt the steam from their mouths. Then she gathered all her strength and yelled, "Boo!" as loud as she could. The trolls jumped. Then they ran off, as fast as their feet could move. From that day on, no troll ever came back to the valley again.

And to this day, people remember her deed. They have even put up a sign. It reads, "Here is where Greta, the Ice Girl, once lived. She drove the trolls away by saying '*Boo!*'"

Name _____

Make a Good Guess continued

Use clues from the story and what you know to answer each question below.

1. What did the people want to do about the trolls?

   They wanted to find a way to stop the trolls or get rid of them. **(2 points)**

   _____

2. What happened to people who were caught by the trolls?

   They had to work for the trolls in their caves. **(2)**

   _____

3. Why did Brother have to do all the family chores?

   Father was hurt badly when he fell. **(2)**

   _____

4. Why did Greta spend so much time knitting?

   She hoped to make money selling hand-knit things, so the family wouldn't

   have to sell a cow. **(2)**

5. At the end, why were no trolls ever seen in the valley again?

   Greta's actions scared them away. **(2)**

   _____

Name _____

Syllabication

If you come across a word you can't pronounce, try dividing the word into **syllables**, or parts of a word that are said out loud as single sounds. Each word below has two syllables. Each can be divided in a different way.

Divide the compound word into two words:

sunrise = sun • rise

Divide the word between two consonants:

village = vil • lage

Write the words below with spaces between the two syllables. Divide them either between the words in a compound word or between two consonants.

1. mirror   mir   ror **(1 point)**

   between two consonants **(1)**

2. nightfall   night   fall **(1)**

   between two words **(1)**

3. poster   pos   ter **(1)**

   between two consonants **(1)**

4. mountain   moun   tain **(1)**

   between two consonants **(1)**

5. downtown   down   town **(1)**

   between two words **(1)**

Assessment Tip: Total **10 Points**

Name _____

More Short Vowels

A short vowel sound is usually spelled with one vowel
followed by a consonant sound.

The /ŏ/ sound is usually spelled *o*, as in l**o**t.

The /ŭ/ sound is usually spelled *u*, as in r**u**b.

▶ Sometimes the /ŭ/ sound is spelled in a different way.
In the starred words *does* and *won*, the /ŭ/ sound is
spelled *oe* and *o*.

Write each Spelling Word under its vowel sound.

Order of answers for each category may vary.

Spelling Words

1. pond
2. luck
3. drop
4. lot
5. rub
6. does*
7. drum
8. sock
9. hunt
10. crop
11. shut
12. won*

/ŏ/ Sound

pond **(1 point)**

drop **(1)**

lot **(1)**

sock **(1)**

crop **(1)**

/ŭ/ Sound

luck **(1)**

rub **(1)**

does **(1)**

drum **(1)**

hunt **(1)**

shut **(1)**

won **(1)**

Assessment Tip: Total **12** Points

Name _____

Spelling Spree

Finding Words Write the Spelling Word hidden in each of these words.

	Spelling Words
	1. pond
	2. luck
	3. drop
	4. lot
	5. rub
	6. does*
	7. drum
	8. sock
	9. hunt
	10. crop
	11. shut
	12. won*

1. shutter   shut **(1 point)**

2. wonderful   won **(1)**

3. plot   lot **(1)**

4. rubber   rub **(1)**

5. doesn't   does **(1)**

6. eardrum   drum **(1)**

Questions Write a Spelling Word to answer each question.

7. What do you wear inside a shoe?

8. What does a farmer grow?

9. What can help you win a game?

10. What body of water is smaller than a lake?

11. What do lions do to get their dinner?

12. What do you call a tiny bead of water?

7. sock **(1 point)**   10. pond **(1)**

8. crop **(1)**   11. hunt **(1)**

9. luck **(1)**   12. drop **(1)**

Assessment Tip: Total **12 Points**

Name _____

Proofreading and Writing

Proofreading Circle the five misspelled Spelling Words below. Then write each word correctly.

The Emperor Praises Mulan

The Emperor welcomed General Mulan to the High Palace today. First, a soldier played a huge (drume). Then the Emperor gave a speech. He told how Mulan was willing to (droppe) everything to join the army. He said the famous general did not win battles by (luk), but by skill and bravery. Now, thanks to Mulan, the war is (wone). No longer (dose) an invading army threaten China. The gates of the Great Wall are safely shut.

Spelling Words

1. pond
2. luck
3. drop
4. lot
5. rub
6. does*
7. drum
8. sock
9. hunt
10. crop
11. shut
12. won*

1. drum **(1 point)**
2. drop **(1)**
3. luck **(1)**
4. won **(1)**
5. does **(1)**

Write a Story Long ago, in a land far away, a brave young girl named Mulan began a dangerous adventure. How would you begin an adventure story? What setting would you use? It could be a dark jungle or a distant planet, or it might be your own neighborhood.

On a separate sheet of paper, write the opening paragraph of an adventure story. Use Spelling Words from the list. Responses will vary. **(5)**

Name _____

Multiple Meaning Words

> **long** *adjective* **1.** Having great length: *a long river.*
> **2.** Lasting for a large amount of time: *a long movie.*
> **3.** Lasting a certain length: *The show was an hour long.*
> ◆ *adverb* Far away in the past: *The dinosaurs lived long ago.*
> ◆ *verb* To wish or want very much: *The children longed for an ice cream cone.*

For each of the following sentences, choose the correct definition of the underlined word. Write the definition on the line.

1. Long ago, a girl named Mulan went into battle.

   far away in the past **(1 point)**

2. A long line of soldiers crossed the mountain.

   having great length **(1)**

3. The town longed for peace to return.

   to wish or want very much **(1)**

4. It was a long way to the Yellow River.

   having great length **(1)**

5. Mulan longed to hear her mother's voice.

   to wish or want very much **(1)**

6. The war was ten years long.

   lasting a certain length **(1)**

Assessment Tip: Total **6** Points

Name _____

Classifying Sentences

Read and classify each sentence. Write *statement*, *question*, *command*, or *exclamation* on the line provided.

1. Why did Mulan fight in the army? question **(1 point)**

2. What an amazing girl she is! exclamation **(1)**

3. Tell me what her journey was like. command **(1)**

4. She was surrounded by many dangers. statement **(1)**

5. Mulan's family and friends were very proud of her.

   statement **(1)**

6. There she goes now! exclamation **(1)**

7. Watch the victory parade. command **(1)**

8. Can you see Mulan at the front of the troops?

   question **(1)**

9. The musicians sing a song about Mulan's

   adventures. statement **(1)**

10. How beautiful the music sounds!

    exclamation **(1)**

Name _____

Arranging Sentences

Arrange these sentences to create an interview with Mulan. Four of the sentences are questions and four are the answers to these questions. On the lines below, write each question followed by its answer. Add the correct end marks.

I dressed in armor	I was terrified at first
Were you afraid	Why did you join the army
My father was too ill to fight	Look at my face and see how
Are you glad to be home	happy I am
	What did you wear

The order of the questions and answers may vary.

1. **Q:** Why did you join the army? **(1 point)**

   A: My father was too ill to fight. **(1)**

2. **Q:** Were you afraid? **(1)**

   A: I was terrified at first! **(1)**

3. **Q:** What did you wear? **(1)**

   A: I dressed in armor. **(1)**

4. **Q:** Are you glad to be home? **(1)**

   A: Look at my face and see how happy I am. **(1)**

Assessment Tip: Total **8 Points**

Name _____

Capitalizing and Punctuating Sentences

Capital letters and punctuation help us to understand writing. Three students decided to act out a scene from *The Ballad of Mulan*. Here is the script they wrote for the scene. Check the capitalization and punctuation of each sentence. Then rewrite the script, using the correct capitalization and punctuation.

Soldier 1: Mulan, is that really you

1. Mulan, is that really you? **(2 points)**

Soldier 2: how is this possible

2. How is this possible? **(2)**

Soldier 1: are you really a girl

3. Are you really a girl? **(2)**

Mulan: yes, I am you have not seen the real me

4. Yes, I am. You have not seen the real me. **(2)**

Soldier 1: you are brave and amazing

5. You are brave and amazing! **(2)**

Soldier 2: what a remarkable girl you are

6. What a remarkable girl you are! **(2)**

Mulan: I had to save my father would you have let me fight if I had dressed as a woman

7. I had to save my father. Would you have let me fight if I had

dressed as a woman? **(2)**

Assessment Tip: Total **14** Points

Name _____

Response Journal

Writing a Response Journal Entry Write about a story you
are reading now. Answer the questions. Use your own ideas.

Title of Story _Responses will vary._ **(1 point)**

How do I feel about what happens in the story?

Responses will vary. **(1)** _____

_____

How do I feel about the main character?

Responses will vary. **(1)** _____

_____

What do I think will happen next in the story?

Responses will vary. **(1)** _____

_____

What puzzles me about the story?

Responses will vary. **(1)** _____

_____

Which character in the story is most like me? Why?

Responses will vary. **(1)** _____

_____

Assessment Tip: Total **6** Points

Name _____

Capitalizing Days and Months

► Begin an entry in your journal with the day or date.
► Begin the name of the day of the week with a capital letter.

     Monday   **T**uesday   **W**ednesday   **T**hursday
     Friday   **S**aturday   **S**unday

► Begin the months of the year with capital letters.

     April 12
     November 24

Write each day or date correctly.

1. wednesday   Wednesday **(1 point)**

2. friday, november 18   Friday, November 18 **(2)**

3. saturday   Saturday **(1)**

4. monday, january 7   Monday, January 7 **(2)**

5. thursday   Thursday **(1)**

6. tuesday, may 8   Tuesday, May 8 **(2)**

7. sunday   Sunday **(1)**

Name _____

Adventure Advertisement

Help rewrite this ad to make it more exciting. Replace the words in parentheses with words from the box. Fill in the blanks with the correct words.

Vocabulary

1. ledges
2. boulders
3. scouted
4. Canyon
5. sheer
6. cauldron
7. rapids

Visit Adventure <u>Canyon **(1 point)**</u> (Valley)! Ride a canoe through <u>rapids **(1)**</u> (fast, tiny waterfalls in a river). Dock your canoe and cross the river by stepping on huge <u>boulders **(1)**</u> (round rocks). Walk past Silver Waterfall, where the river looks like a boiling <u>cauldron **(1)**</u> (kettle). After you've <u>scouted **(1)**</u> (searched out) a path, hike to the top of the waterfall. Be careful! To climb the <u>sheer **(1)**</u> (very steep) rock walls, you'll have to find <u>ledges **(1)**</u> (rock shelves) on the sides of the cliffs.

Answer the following question. (Hint: If you need help, look at pages 92–93 in your textbook.)

What is a waterfall?

Possible response: Water falling where there is a sudden
_____
drop in the level of a river or a stream. **(1)**

Assessment Tip: Total **8** Points

Name _____

Cause and Effect Chart

Cause (Why does it happen?)	Effect (What happens?)
They don't want to walk in the poison oak. **(2 points)**	They wade through the cold water.
The water going over the falls makes a roaring noise. **(2)**	They hear a roaring sound.
A wild animal comes down to the creek to drink.	The boy hears a growl and a rustle in the brush. **(2)**
The boy is happy when he reaches the top.	He slaps five, does a dance, and shouts to his parents. **(2)**
"The Dancer" reminds the boy of the waterfall and the camping trip.	It makes his heart feel big and wild. **(2)**

Name _____

Finish the Story

Complete each of the sentences with details from
The Waterfall.

1. In July the boy and his family backpack far up a creek.
   (1 point)

2. The family finds a waterfall that is higher _____
   than the pines around it. **(1)**

3. When the sun gets hot, the family keeps cool by
   tying leaves on their heads with vines and by wading in
   the rapids. **(2)**

4. The next day, the boy and his brother climb _____
   up to the top of the falls. **(2)**

5. As his parents climb up the steep rocks, the boy feels
   anxious and proud. **(2)**

6. The boy wants to bring the driftwood home because
   Answers will vary: it reminds him of the adventure; it
   reminds him of the exciting climb and his dance at the top
   of the falls. **(2)**

Assessment Tip: Total **10** Points

Name _____

Causes and Effects

**Read the story. Think about what happens and why.
Then complete the chart on the next page.**

The Tornado

A rooster crowed, waking Lucy Sunders from a deep sleep. She usually popped out of bed like buttons pop off a shirt, but today she was tired. She had stayed up late last night reading.

Lucy looked out her window. The sky was a funny yellow-gray, and there were no sounds. Then, across the fields, Lucy saw a whirling dust cloud. It grew bigger and bigger. A tornado was coming!

Lucy raced down the stairs, shouting, "Mama, Mama — a tornado!"

Mrs. Sunders checked the sky. Then she grabbed the baby from his swing. "Run! Run to the root cellar!" she shouted.

Lucy and her mother ran through the yard, and Lucy pulled open the cellar door. She hurried down the steps. Her mother locked the door and followed her into the darkness.

Quickly Mrs. Sunders lit the old lamp, and the light glowed warmly. Lucy sighed. They were safe now. Everything would be all right.

Name _____

Causes and Effects continued

In each box, write a cause or an effect from the story.

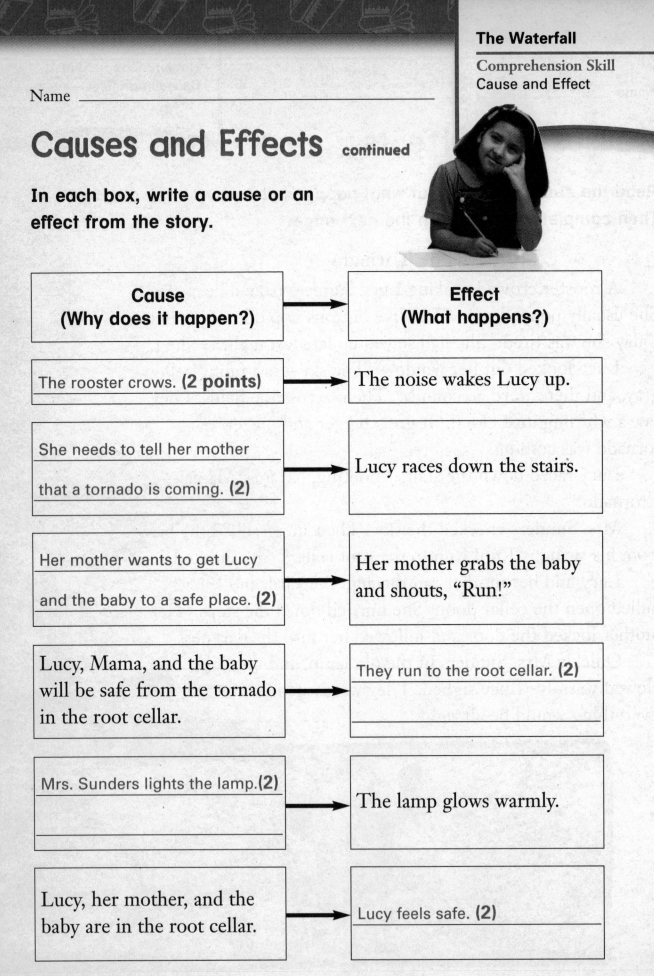

Cause (Why does it happen?)	Effect (What happens?)
The rooster crows. **(2 points)**	The noise wakes Lucy up.
She needs to tell her mother that a tornado is coming. **(2)**	Lucy races down the stairs.
Her mother wants to get Lucy and the baby to a safe place. **(2)**	Her mother grabs the baby and shouts, "Run!"
Lucy, Mama, and the baby will be safe from the tornado in the root cellar.	They run to the root cellar. **(2)**
Mrs. Sunders lights the lamp. **(2)**	The lamp glows warmly.
Lucy, her mother, and the baby are in the root cellar.	Lucy feels safe. **(2)**

42   Theme 1: **Off to Adventure!**
Assessment Tip: Total **12** Points

Name _____

Add the Ending

► For words that end with a vowel and a single
  consonant, double the consonant before adding
  -ed or *-ing*.

  grip + p + ed = gripped   swim + m + ing = swimming

**Read the clues for the puzzle. For each one, choose
a word from the box with the same meaning as the
word in dark type. Complete the puzzle by adding
-ed or *-ing* to the word from the box.**

Word Bank

sip
drag
trap
drop
swim
dig
rip

Across

4. My brother and I **pulled**
   the heavy branches.
5. The mountain lion **tore**
   open the tent.
6. The raccoon **drank** water
   from the stream.
7. The boys are **moving** in
   the cold, clear water.

Down

1. My foot was **caught**
   between two rocks!
2. Can you hear the water
   falling?
3. The bear is **searching**
   under the log for grubs.

Name _____

The Vowel-Consonant-*e* Pattern

The long *a, i, o,* and *u* sounds are shown as /ā/, /ī/, /ō/, and /ōō/. When you hear these sounds, remember that they are often spelled with the vowel-consonant-*e* pattern.

   /ā/ **save**   /ī/ **life**   /ō/ sm**oke**   /ōō/ h**uge**

► In the starred words *come* and *love*, the *o*-consonant-*e* pattern spells the /ŭ/ sound.

Write each Spelling Word under its vowel sound.
Order of answers for each category may vary.

Spelling Words

1. smoke
2. huge
3. save
4. life
5. wide
6. come*
7. mine
8. grade
9. smile
10. note
11. cube
12. love*

/ā/ or /ī/ Sound

save **(1 point)**

life **(1)**

wide **(1)**

mine **(1)**

grade **(1)**

smile **(1)**

/ō/ or /ōō/ Sound

smoke **(1)**

huge **(1)**

note **(1)**

cube **(1)**

No long vowel Sound

come **(1)**

love **(1)**

Spelling Spree

Book Titles Write the Spelling Word that best completes each book title. Remember to use capital letters. (1 point each)

1. Sing Every _Note_____ by B. A. Soprano

2. I _Love_____ My Cats and Dogs by

   Ima Petowner

3. Dinosaurs Were _Huge_____! by Sy N. Tific

4. Live Your _Life_____ to the Fullest by

   Hy Lee Adventurous

5. _Come_____ to My Party by U. R. Invited

Puzzle Play Write a Spelling Word for each clue. Then write the circled letters in order to spell something you might see over a waterfall.

Spelling Words

1. smoke
2. huge
3. save
4. life
5. wide
6. come*
7. mine
8. grade
9. smile
10. note
11. cube
12. love*

6. a year of school _g_ (r) _a_ _d_ _e_ (1)

7. to keep for a while _s_ (a) _v_ _e_ (1)

8. a happy expression _s_ _m_ (i) _l_ _e_ (1)

9. belongs to me _m_ _i_ (n) _e_ (1)

10. one shape for ice _c_ _u_ (b) _e_ (1)

11. fire can cause it _s_ _m_ (o) _k_ _e_ (1)

12. opposite of narrow (w) _i_ _d_ _e_ (1)

_r_ _a_ _i_ _n_ _b_ _o_ _w_

Assessment Tip: Total **12** Points

Name _____

Proofreading and Writing

Proofreading Circle the five misspelled Spelling Words in the following notice. Then write each word correctly.

Attention All Visitors

Our wilderness areas are home to many kinds of animal and plant (lif). They provide nesting areas for (huje) numbers of birds. People (com) from cities and towns all over the world to camp and hike in the wilderness. Show your respect and (luv) for the natural world. The children of the future must have the chance to enjoy these (wid) open spaces too.

1. life **(2 points)**
2. huge **(2)**
3. come **(2)**
4. love **(2)**
5. wide **(2)**

Write a Journal Entry Think about a special time you had outdoors. Where were you? Was it a field trip? A family outing? Or maybe a block party?

On a separate sheet of paper, describe where you were and what was special about the experience. Use Spelling Words from the list. Responses will vary. **(5)**

Assessment Tip: Total **15** Points

Name _____

Entry Words

Suppose the boy wrote this letter. Decide whether each underlined word would be an entry word in a dictionary or part of an entry. Write the word in the correct column.

Dear Malcolm,

Our <u>camping</u> trip was great! We <u>backpacked</u> across a creek and set up our tents near the water. Then we had a <u>cookout</u> and watched the stars. We heard <u>growling</u> outside our tent, and I was scared. The next morning, we found tracks outside our tent. Dad said it was a <u>mountain lion</u>! The best part of the trip was when we <u>climbed</u> to the top of a huge waterfall. My <u>brother</u> and I were really proud, especially when Mom and Dad made it to the top! You'll have to see the great <u>souvenir</u> I brought back with me the next time you visit.

Your friend

Entry Word	**Part of an Entry**
cookout **(1 point)**	camping **(1)**
mountain lion **(1)**	backpacked **(1)**
brother **(1)**	growling **(1)**
souvenir **(1)**	climbed **(1)**

Name _____

Connecting Subjects and Predicates

Read the sentence parts. Write S next to each subject. Write P next to each predicate. Then put the parts together to write six sentences. Write your sentences on the lines below.

a distant owl **S**	block our path **P**
the pounding water **S**	crashes against the rocky
carries her own backpack **P**	canyon **P**
my father **S**	puts on his hiking boots **P**
the squirrels and	a few giant boulders **S**
chipmunks **S**	my sister **S**
hoots to the moon **P**	collect food on the ground **P**

1. The pounding water crashes against the rocky canyon. **(2 points)**

2. My sister carries her own backpack. **(2)**

3. My father puts on his hiking boots. **(2)**

4. A distant owl hoots to the moon. **(2)**

5. A few giant boulders block our path. **(2)**

6. The squirrels and chipmunks collect food on the ground. **(2)**

Assessment Tip: Total **12** Points

Name _____

Combining Subjects and Predicates

Combine each pair of sentences. Then write the new sentence on the line.

1. The sun shines. The sun heats the air.

   The sun shines and heats the air. **(2 points)**

2. My brother sees some animals. I see some animals.

   My brother and I see some animals. **(2)**

3. The foxes run away. The deer run away.

   The foxes and the deer run away. **(2)**

4. We follow the trail. We find a cave.

   We follow the trail and find a cave. **(2)**

5. The cave is dark. The cave is large.

   The cave is dark and large. **(2)**

6. We find our flashlight. We turn it on.

   We find our flashlight and turn it on. **(2)**

7. Bats live in caves. Bears live in caves.

   Bats and bears live in caves. **(2)**

8. Mother reminds us to be safe. Father reminds us to be safe.

   Mother and father remind us to be safe. **(2)**

Assessment Tip: Total **16** Points

Name _____

Subjects and Predicates

Write the complete subject and the complete predicate of each of the following sentences in the correct column.

1. We went camping.
2. Our new tent is very light.
3. The sunset was beautiful.
4. A full moon glows.
5. My sister woke up at sunrise.
6. She cooked breakfast over the campfire.
7. Our entire family walked to the canyon.
8. The rocky canyon is full of dangerous places.
9. My father and I spotted the waterfall.
10. The rushing water splashed our faces.

Subjects	Predicates
We **(1 point)**	went camping. **(1)**
Our new tent **(1)**	is very light. **(1)**
The sunset **(1)**	was beautiful. **(1)**
A full moon **(1)**	glows. **(1)**
My sister **(1)**	woke up at sunrise. **(1)**
She **(1)**	cooked breakfast over the campfire. **(1)**
Our entire family **(1)**	walked to the canyon. **(1)**
The rocky canyon **(1)**	is full of dangerous places. **(1)**
My father and I **(1)**	spotted the waterfall. **(1)**
The rushing water **(1)**	splashed our faces. **(1)**

Assessment Tip: Total **20 Points**

Name _____

Reasons and Facts

Use this page to plan your explanation. Then number
your reasons or facts in the order you will use them.

Topic: **(2 points)** _____

_____

_____

Topic Sentence: **(2)** _____

_____

_____

Reason/Fact: **(2)** _____

_____

_____

Reason/Fact: **(2)** _____

_____

_____

Reason/Fact: **(2)** _____

_____

_____

Reason/Fact: **(2)** _____

_____

_____

Name _____

Improving Your Writing

► Sometimes questions can be changed into statements by moving the words around.
Are the children's parents good climbers?
The children's parents are good climbers.

► Sometimes words must be added, removed, or changed to make a question into a statement.
Did most readers like the story?
Most readers liked the story.

► Changing the question on a test into a statement can help you write a good topic sentence and focus your ideas.
Why is climbing exciting?
There are several reason why climbing is exciting.

Change each question into a statement.
Answers will vary. Possible answers are given.

1. What are some of the family's favorite activities?

   The family has several favorite activities. **(2 points)**

2. Did everyone in the class like the action story?

   Everyone in the class liked the action story. **(2)**

3. Who are the main characters in this story?

   There are several main characters in this story. [Names of

   characters] are the main characters in this story. **(2)**

4. Why is swimming under a waterfall fun?

   Swimming under a waterfall is fun for a number of reasons. **(2)**

5. What types of movies does their family like to see?

   Their family likes to see several types of movies. **(2)**

Assessment Tip: Total **10** Points

Name _____

Choosing the Best Answer

Use the test-taking strategies and tips you have learned to help you answer these questions. You may go back to *The Waterfall* if you need to. This practice will help you when you take this kind of test.

Read each question. Fill in the circle next to the best answer.

1 Why did the family wade through the cold water?

  ○ They wanted to cool off in the heat of the summer.

  ○ The rocks along the creek were too slippery to climb.

  ○ They were looking for the waterfall.

  ● There was poison oak along the banks of the creek. **(5 points)**

2 What was the first clue the family had that a waterfall was nearby?

  ● They heard a roaring sound. **(5)**

  ○ They saw a rainbow in the sky.

  ○ They felt the mist spray on their faces.

  ○ They saw a steep rock slope.

3 Why did Dad say, "End of the road," when the family got to the waterfall?

  ○ The trail they were on ended at the waterfall.

  ● He thought the waterfall was too dangerous to climb. **(5)**

  ○ The waterfall was as far as he wanted the family to go.

  ○ Once they got to the waterfall, he was ready to go home.

Name _____

Choosing the Best Answer

continued

4   What happened that made the older boy feel scared before
    he fell asleep?

   ● He heard something in the brush. **(5)**

   ○ He thought about climbing the waterfall.

   ○ He saw a wild animal near the camp.

   ○ He thought the family was lost.

5   What made the tracks near the family's camp?

   ○ a deer

   ○ a grizzly bear

   ○ a wolf

   ● a mountain lion **(5)**

6   What did the family decide to do after finding the tracks?

   ○ go back the way they had come

   ○ return home

   ● climb the waterfall **(5)**

   ○ contact the park ranger

Assessment Tip: Total **30** Points

Name _____

Spelling Review

Write Spelling Words from the list to answer the questions. Order of answers in each category may vary.

Spelling Words

1–17. Which seventeen words have short vowels?

1. drum **(1 point)**

2. last **(1)**

3. drop **(1)**

4. class **(1)**

5. left **(1)**

6. mix **(1)**

7. send **(1)**

8. smell **(1)**

9. stick **(1)**

10. thick **(1)**

11. hunt **(1)**

12. thin **(1)**

13. lot **(1)**

14. pond **(1)**

15. sock **(1)**

16. luck **(1)**

17. shut **(1)**

18–25. Which eight words have the vowel-consonant-*e* pattern?

18. huge **(1)**

19. wide **(1)**

20. save **(1)**

21. note **(1)**

22. grade **(1)**

23. cube **(1)**

24. life **(1)**

25. smile **(1)**

Spelling Words

1. drum
2. huge
3. last
4. drop
5. class
6. left
7. wide
8. mix
9. send
10. save
11. smell
12. stick
13. note
14. thick
15. hunt
16. thin
17. grade
18. lot
19. cube
20. pond
21. life
22. sock
23. luck
24. shut
25. smile

Name _____

Spelling Spree

Book Titles Write the Spelling Word that best completes each funny book title. Remember to use capital letters.

Example: *The Great _____ from Planet X*
by I. C. Starrs _____Escape_____

1. *Put an Ice _____ in My Glass and Other Science Experiments* by Sy N. Seen

2. *A _____ Is a Frown Upside Down* by Mary Timz

3. *My First Day in _____ 3: A True Story* by Ima Newcomer

4. *The Mystery in the Third Grade _____* by Minnie Klooz

5. *_____ Us a Post Card* by U. R. A. Riter

6. *Do I _____ Cookies?* by I. M. Hungree

1. <u>Cube</u> **(1 point)**

2. <u>Smile</u> **(1)**

3. <u>Grade</u> **(1)**

4. <u>Class</u> **(1)**

5. <u>Send</u> **(1)**

6. <u>Smell</u> **(1)**

One, Two, Three! Write the Spelling Word that belongs in each group.

7. piano, guitar, <u>drum</u> **(1)**

8. big, large, <u>huge</u> **(1)**

9. lake, river, <u>pond</u> **(1)**

10. stir, blend, <u>mix</u> **(1)**

11. shirt, shoe, <u>sock</u> **(1)**

12. twig, branch, <u>stick</u> **(1)**

56   Theme 1: **Off to Adventure!**
Assessment Tip: Total **12** Points

Proofreading and Writing

Proofreading **Circle the five misspelled Spelling Words below. Then write each word correctly.**

January 12—Today I went on a treasure (hunte.) I spent a (lott) of time looking for the treasure in a (thic) grove of trees and near the pond. I didn't have any (luk.) Maybe somebody will (drap) a clue that I will find!

1. hunt **(1 point)**

4. luck **(1)**

2. lot **(1)**

5. drop **(1)**

3. thick **(1)**

A Newspaper Article **Write a Spelling Word that means the same as each underlined word or words.**

Jeremy is a 6. <u>skinny</u> boy in Mr. Boyd's third grade 7. <u>group</u>. All of his 8. <u>years of being</u> Jeremy had heard about a buried treasure. One day he found a 9. <u>short letter</u> in his attic. It was all that was 10. <u>still around</u> of his grandfather's things. He 11. <u>closed</u> the door and read. "Keep your eyes 12. <u>all the way</u> open," it said. "Look under the 13. <u>final</u> tree in the yard." There Jeremy found a journal that he will 14. <u>keep</u>.

6. thin

9. note

12. wide

7. class

10. left

13. last

8. life

11. shut

14. save

Write a Letter **On a separate sheet of paper, write to a friend about a buried treasure you hope to find. Use the Spelling Review Words.** Responses will vary. **(6)**

Name _____

Celebrating Traditions

Describe a tradition that you celebrate. When do you celebrate it? Who shares the celebration with you? What is your favorite part of this tradition? (5 points)

_____
_____
_____
_____
_____
_____
_____
_____

List any traditions you would like to learn about.

(5) _____
_____
_____
_____
_____

Name _____

Celebrating Traditions

Fill in the chart as you read the stories.
Sample answers shown.

The Keeping Quilt

What tradition is celebrated in this selection?

Polacco celebrates family events by using a quilt that is passed down from generation to generation. **(2 points)**

Why is this tradition important to those who celebrate it?

Polacco's quilt reminds her of the difficult and wonderful events that have happened in her family over the years. **(3)**

Anthony Reynoso: Born to Rope

What tradition is celebrated in this selection?

Anthony celebrates roping by performing at community festivals. **(2)**

Why is this tradition important to those who celebrate it?

Anthony is able to learn a difficult skill from his father, and to share it with the whole community. **(3)**

The Talking Cloth

What tradition is celebrated in this selection?

Amber learns about the printed cloth that celebrates her heritage and how it can express the character of different family members. **(2)**

Why is this tradition important to those who celebrate it?

The Talking Cloth allows Amber to learn more about herself, her history, and the other people in her family. **(3)**

Dancing Rainbows

What tradition is celebrated in this selection?

Curt learns about the dancing traditions of his ancestors. **(2)**

Why is this tradition important to those who celebrate it?

Curt learns about his ancestors and gets to spend time with his grandfather. **(3)**

Assessment Tip: Total **20** Points

Name _____

Quilt Crossword

Write the word that matches each clue in the puzzle. Use the vocabulary words for help.

Vocabulary

border
gathering
needles
scraps
sewn
threaded

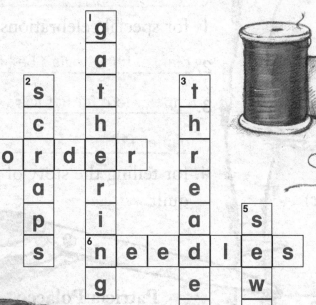

Across

4. edge **(2 points)**

6. tools for sewing **(2)**

Down

1. coming together **(2)**

2. leftover pieces **(2)**

3. passed through the eye
   of a needle **(2)**

5. put together with a
   needle and thread **(2)**

Name _____

Author's Family Chart

Accept varied responses.

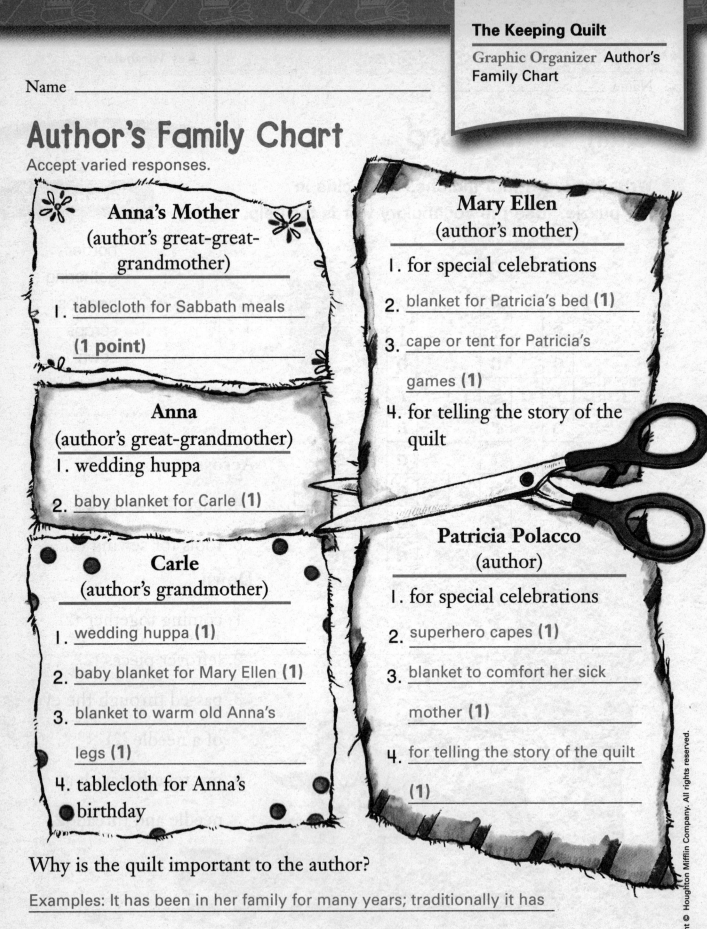

Anna's Mother
(author's great-great-
grandmother)
_____

1. tablecloth for Sabbath meals

(1 point)

Anna
(author's great-grandmother)
1. wedding huppa

2. baby blanket for Carle **(1)**

Carle
(author's grandmother)
_____

1. wedding huppa **(1)**

2. baby blanket for Mary Ellen **(1)**

3. blanket to warm old Anna's

legs **(1)**

4. tablecloth for Anna's
birthday

Mary Ellen
(author's mother)
_____

1. for special celebrations

2. blanket for Patricia's bed **(1)**

3. cape or tent for Patricia's

games **(1)**

4. for telling the story of the
quilt

Patricia Polacco
(author)

1. for special celebrations

2. superhero capes **(1)**

3. blanket to comfort her sick

mother **(1)**

4. for telling the story of the quilt

(1)

Why is the quilt important to the author?

Examples: It has been in her family for many years; traditionally it has

been used for special family celebrations. **(2)**

Name _____

Piece It Together

Finish each statement with details from *The Keeping Quilt*.

Answers may vary. Examples are given.

1. Anna's mother decides to make the quilt because

   it will be a good way to remember the home and family they left in

   Russia. **(2 points)**

2. When Carle grows up, Great-Gramma Anna passes the quilt on to her. She

   uses it and passes it on to Mary Ellen, her daughter. **(2)**

   _____

3. Over the years, people in the family use the quilt as

   a wedding huppa, a baby blanket, a pretend cape, and a tablecloth

   for celebrations. **(2)**

4. Mary Ellen tells her daughter (the author) whose

   clothes were used to make the quilt. **(2)**

   _____

5. Mary Ellen also is lucky enough to tell the story of the quilt to

   her grandchildren and great-grandchildren. **(2)**

   _____

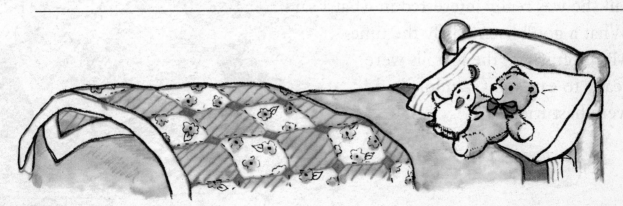

Name _____

An Author's View

Read the story. Then finish the chart on the next page.

Foxtails

When I first saw Grandma Sorensen in her doorway, she seemed ten feet tall and skinny! She frowned as she squinted into the sun and watched our car. Would I like her?

In the living room, Grandma Sorensen gave each of us a big hug. Then she and Mom began talking. Soon they were laughing about things Mom did as a girl. Once she fell out of their apple tree and broke her arm. Then Grandma told how she too had fallen out of an apple tree and broken her arm. That was when she was a girl in Denmark. I said, "I'm never going to climb apple trees!" Grandma laughed.

Later, after Mom had left for a meeting, Grandma suggested that we make my mother a treat, the one she loved best at my age. In the kitchen, Grandma let me mix flour, sugar, eggs, butter, and vanilla together to make a stiff dough. Then she showed me how to pinch off a small piece of dough, roll it, and twist it into a "foxtail." She didn't mind that I made the tails a bit crooked.

As we worked, Grandma asked me about school and what I wanted to be when I grew up. From her questions I could tell she was really interested in what I said. What a good listener! By the time Mom returned, the foxtails were ready to eat, and Grandma and I were best friends.

Name _____

An Author's View continued

Use story details to finish this chart. Tell how the author feels about her grandmother. Answers may vary.

Scene	Details About Grandma	Author's Feelings About Grandma
The Doorway	1. She seems ten feet tall. (1 point) 2. She frowns as she watches the car. (1)	She seems big and scary. (1)
The Living Room	1. She happily remembers tales from the past. (1) 2. She laughs often. (1)	She enjoys remembering the past. (1)
The Kitchen	1. She lets the author make foxtails. (1) 2. She's really interested in what the author says. (1)	She's patient and a good listener. (1)

If you met Grandma Sorensen, do you think you would like her? Why or why not? Use complete sentences.

Answers will vary. (1) _____

_____

_____

Name _____

Compound Mix-up

Write a compound word to match each picture clue.
Each word is made up of two words from the Word Bank.

Word Bank

dog	bug	pot	lady	flower	flag
fly	dragon	tooth	rain	fish	bow
house	brush	pole	moon	star	light

dragonfly **(1 point)**   doghouse **(1)**   flagpole **(1)**

toothbrush **(1)**   ladybug **(1)**   starfish **(1)**

moonlight **(1)**   rainbow **(1)**   flowerpot **(1)**

Combine two words from the Word Bank to make a new
compound word. Answers will vary.

(1) _____

Assessment Tip: Total **10** Points

Name _____

More Long Vowel Spellings

To spell a word with the /ā/ sound, remember that /ā/ can be spelled *ai* or *ay*. To spell a word with the /ē/ sound, remember that /ē/ can be spelled *ea* or *ee*.

| /ā/ | ai, ay | p**ai**nt, cl**ay** |
| /ē/ | ea, ee | l**ea**ve, f**ee**l |

► In the starred words *neighbor*, *eight*, and *weigh*, the /ā/ sound is spelled *eigh*.

Write each Spelling Word under its vowel sound.

Order of answers for each category may vary.

Spelling Words

1. paint
2. clay
3. feel
4. leave
5. neighbor*
6. eight*
7. seem
8. speak
9. paid
10. lay
11. need
12. weigh*

/ā/ Sound

paint **(1 point)**

clay **(1)**

neighbor **(1)**

eight **(1)**

paid **(1)**

lay **(1)**

weigh **(1)**

/ē/ Sound

feel **(1)**

leave **(1)**

seem **(1)**

speak **(1)**

need **(1)**

Name _____

Spelling Spree

Fill in the Blank **Write the Spelling Word that best completes each sentence.**

1. I whisper when I need to _____ softly.

2. My _____ lives across the street.

3. I stand on the scale when I want to _____ myself.

4. My brother formed a bowl out of _____.

5. I set up my easel when I want to _____.

6. One more than seven is _____.

7. I don't want to stay, so I will _____.

1. speak **(1 point)**

2. neighbor **(1)**

3. weigh **(1)**

4. clay **(1)**

5. paint **(1)**

6. eight **(1)**

7. leave **(1)**

Letter Swap **Write a Spelling Word by changing the first letter of each word.**

8. peel   feel **(1)**

9. maid   paid **(1)**

10. seed   need **(1)**

11. say   lay **(1)**

12. teem   seem **(1)**

68   Theme 2: **Celebrating Traditions**
Assessment Tip: Total **12** Points

Name _____

Proofreading and Writing

Proofreading Circle the five misspelled Spelling Words in this invitation. Then write each word correctly.

Dear New Neighbor,

    Please join me and some of the other tenants in the building for a quilting party. I have enough needles and thread for (eaght) helpers. You don't (ned) to be a sewing expert. The work will (seam) easy, and we will all get to know one another. Later we will have tea and cake. The party will be in my apartment next Monday evening. If you are interested, (spek) to me soon. If you prefer, you can (leve) a note in my mailbox instead.

        Sincerely,
        Natasha Pushkin

Spelling Words

1. paint
2. clay
3. feel
4. leave
5. neighbor*
6. eight*
7. seem
8. speak
9. paid
10. lay
11. need
12. weigh*

1. eight **(2 points)**

2. need **(2)**

3. seem **(2)**

4. speak **(2)**

5. leave **(2)**

Write a Description If you were going to design a quilt like the one in the story, what would it look like?

On a separate sheet of paper, write about a quilt you would design. Tell what material you would use and why. Use Spelling Words from the list. Responses will vary. **(2)**

Name _____

Word Family Reunion

Select the words that belong to the word family for "back."
Then arrange the words on the chart and define each one.
Check your work in a dictionary.

Word Bank

backward	bacteria	backyard	bachelor	backboard
backbone	backfire	background	backpack	backup

The Back Family

Word	Meaning
1. backward **(1 point)**	in the opposite direction **(1)**
2. backyard **(1)**	yard at the back of the house **(1)**
3. backboard **(1)**	flat board used in basketball **(1)**
4. backbone **(1)**	the spine **(1)**
5. backfire **(1)**	to have a bad or unexpected result **(1)**
6. background **(1)**	part of the scene not in the front **(1)**
7. backpack **(1)**	bag worn on the back **(1)**
8. backup **(1)**	support or help **(1)**

Assessment Tip: Total **16** Points

Name _____

In Search of Common Nouns

Circle the common noun or nouns in each group of words.

1. big (room) **(1)**

2. (quilt) sewed (needle) **(1)**

3. (house) talk enjoy (people) **(1)**

4. (blanket) warm (sister) (friend) **(1)**

5. happy silly (story) angry **(1)**

6. curious (city) cheerful sad **(1)**

Write the circled nouns in the correct square below.

Persons

people **(1 point)** _____

sister **(1)** _____

friend **(1)** _____

Things

quilt **(1)** _____

needle **(1)** _____

blanket **(1)** _____

story **(1)** _____

Places

room **(1)** _____

house **(1)** _____

city **(1)** _____

Name _____

Common Nouns in Signs

**Find the common nouns in the report. Write each common
noun in the correct exhibit room below.**

A Visit to the Museum

My friends and I visited a museum. There we saw a
collection of wonderful old quilts. Some of them were
made by pioneers. Many of the blankets showed children,
flowers, and trees. One showed all fifty states.

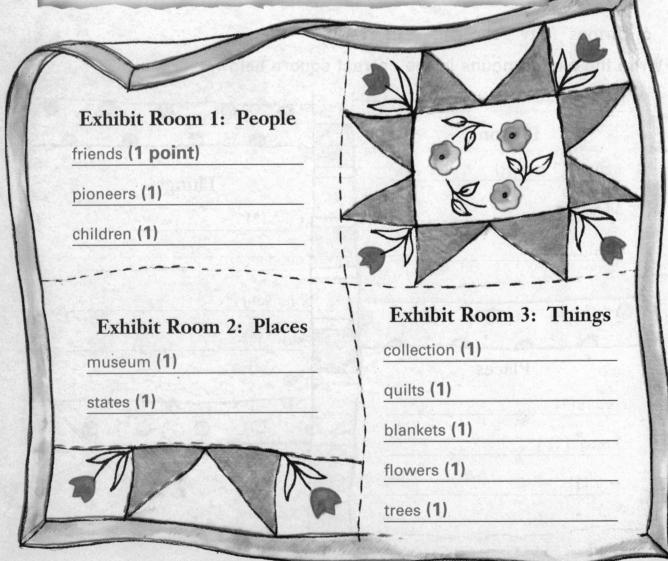

Exhibit Room 1: People

friends **(1 point)**

pioneers **(1)**

children **(1)**

Exhibit Room 2: Places

museum **(1)**

states **(1)**

Exhibit Room 3: Things

collection **(1)**

quilts **(1)**

blankets **(1)**

flowers **(1)**

trees **(1)**

Assessment Tip: Total **10** Points

Name _____

Commas in a Series

Proofread each sentence. Add commas to separate each series of three or more words. Remove all unnecessary commas.

1. Our attic is filled with boxes bags and books.

   Our attic is filled with boxes, bags, and books. **(1 point)**

2. I found my great-grandfather's hat gloves and cane.

   I found my great-grandfather's hat, gloves, and cane. **(1)**

3. The cane was carved with tigers lions and elephants.

   The cane was carved with tigers, lions, and elephants. **(1)**

4. I also found old journals photographs and drawings.

   I also found old journals, photographs, and drawings. **(1)**

5. One photograph shows my aunt uncle and cousin.

   One photograph shows my aunt, uncle, and cousin. **(1)**

6. My great-grandmother lived on a farm with chickens cows horses and pigs.

   My great-grandmother lived on a farm with chickens, cows,

   horses, and pigs. **(1)**

7. In her diary, she described her, friends relatives and visitors.

   In her diary, she described her friends, relatives, and visitors. **(1)**

8. Her hopes wishes and dreams, bring every page to life.

   Her hopes, wishes, and dreams bring every page to life. **(1)**

Name _____

Paragraphs That Compare and Contrast

Use the chart on this page to help you plan paragraphs that compare and contrast. Write what the paragraphs will be about. Write two or three interesting details that show how the people, places, and things are alike. Then write how they are different. Use the details you record in your writing.

What I Will Compare and Contrast

(Answers will vary.)

_____

_____

How They Are Alike	How They Are Different
1. **(1 point)** _____	1. **(1)** _____
_____	_____
2. **(1)** _____	2. **(1)** _____
_____	_____
3. **(1)** _____	3. **(1)** _____
_____	_____

Write your paragraphs that compare and contrast on a separate sheet of paper. Include the details you wrote above. **(4 points)**

Assessment Tip: Total **10** Points

Name _____

Sentence Combining

► Connect two related sentences with a comma and a joining word to make a compound sentence.

► Use a comma and the word *and* to create a compound sentence that makes a comparison.

   Example: The gifts were part of the women's bouquets, **and** each gift was a symbol of something important for a good life.

► Use a comma and the word *but* to create a compound sentence that makes a contrast.

   Example: At the first weddings, the women wore wedding dresses, **but** later some women wore suits.

Write a compound sentence. Combine the sentences with a comma and the joining word in parentheses ( ).

1. The women loved the keeping quilt. They used it to keep their family's traditions alive. (and)

   The women loved the keeping quilt, and they used it to keep their

   family's traditions alive. **(2 points)**

2. The women's weddings were alike in some ways. They were also different. (but)

   The women's weddings were alike in some ways,

   but they were also different. **(2)**

3. The quilt was used as a cape. It was used as a huppa too. (and)

   The quilt was used as a cape, and it was used as a huppa too. **(2)**

Revising Your Instructions

Reread your instructions. What do you need to make them better? Use this page to help you decide. Put a checkmark in the box for each sentence that describes your instructions.

Rings the Bell!

☐ The goal of my instructions is clearly stated.

☐ The steps are clear and in the right sequence.

☐ The information that I presented is complete. I included all the necessary details.

☐ I used exact words to make my directions as precise as possible.

Getting Stronger

☐ I could make the goal of the instructions clearer.

☐ My steps aren't always clear. The sequence may need work.

☐ I need to add some important information.

☐ I could add exact words to improve my instructions.

Try Harder

☐ The goal of my instructions is not stated.

☐ The steps aren't clear, and they are out of order.

☐ I left out some very important information.

☐ I need to use more exact words.

Name _____

Using Exact Nouns

Circle the letter of the noun that best replaces each underlined word or phrase.

1. Do you want to be a movie <u>person who acts</u>?

   a. lawyer　　　b. watcher　　(c.) star **(1 point)**　d. Venus

2. First, you need to have a good head of <u>fuzzy stuff</u>.

   (a.) hair **(1)**　　b. ears　　　c. smile　　　d. connections

3. Then, you need some cool clothes and a pair of dark <u>eye things</u>.

   a. pupils　　　b. carrots　　c. cups　　　(d.) sunglasses **(1)**

4. Next, you need a big, fancy house with a <u>big thing of water</u>.

   a. garage　　　b. door　　(c.) pool **(1)**　　d. yard

5. You'll need to eat at all the best <u>eating places</u>.

   (a.) restaurants **(1)**　b. stations　　c. rinks　　　d. garages

6. Of course, you need to have an agent and a <u>person who represents you legally</u>.

   a. judge　　　b. sheriff　　(c.) lawyer **(1)**　　d. partner

7. Do you need any actual acting <u>stuff</u>?

   a. manners　　(b.) talent **(1)**　　c. rules　　　d. clothes

8. "It helps, but it's not a must," say all the top Hollywood movie <u>leaders</u>.

   a. sleepers　　b. sellers　　c. drivers　　(d.) directors **(1)**

Name _____

Spelling Words

Look for spelling patterns you have learned to help you remember the Spelling Words on this page. Think about the parts that you find hard to spell.

Write the missing letters and apostrophe in the Spelling Words below.

1. n <u>o</u> <u>w</u> **(1 point)**

2. o <u>f</u> <u>f</u> **(1)**

3. f <u>o</u> r **(1)**

4. <u>a</u> <u>l</u> most **(1)**

5. <u>a</u> <u>l</u> so **(1)**

6. can <u>'</u> <u>t</u> **(1)**

7. ca <u>n</u> <u>n</u> ot **(1)**

8. ab <u>o</u> <u>u</u> t **(1)**

9. <u>a</u> <u>l</u> ways **(1)**

10. <u>t</u> <u>o</u> day **(1)**

11. unt <u>i</u> <u>l</u> **(1)**

12. ag <u>a</u> <u>i</u> n **(1)**

Spelling Words

1. now
2. off
3. for
4. almost
5. also
6. can't
7. cannot
8. about
9. always
10. today
11. until
12. again

Study List **On another sheet of paper, write each Spelling Word. Check the list to be sure you spell each word correctly.** Order of words may vary. **(2)**

Assessment Tip: Total **14** Points

Name _____

Spelling Spree

Word Switch **For each sentence, write a Spelling Word to take the place of the underlined word or words.**

1. Let's go ride the roller coaster <u>another time</u>!
2. I'm in a real hurry, so I can't talk <u>at this time</u>.
3. Sofia <u>every time</u> has a box of raisins in her lunch.
4. My mom said that you can come to the beach <u>too</u>, if you want.
5. It's been <u>not quite</u> three years since we had a snowstorm.
6. They said on the radio that <u>the current day</u> is the first day of fall.

1. <u>again **(1 point)**</u>
2. <u>now **(1)**</u>
3. <u>always **(1)**</u>
4. <u>also **(1)**</u>
5. <u>almost **(1)**</u>
6. <u>today **(1)**</u>

Letter Math **Add and subtract letters from the words below to make Spelling Words. Write the new words.**

7. foot – ot + r = <u>for **(1)**</u>

8. cart – rt + n't = <u>can't **(1)**</u>

9. able – le + out = <u>about **(1)**</u>

10. order – rder + ff = <u>off **(1)**</u>

11. canned – ed + ot = <u>cannot **(1)**</u>

12. unit – it + til = <u>until **(1)**</u>

Name _____

Proofreading and Writing

Proofreading Find and circle the four misspelled Spelling Words in this poster. Then write each word correctly.

1. now
2. off
3. for
4. almost
5. also
6. can't
7. cannot
8. about
9. always
10. today
11. until
12. again

Brazilian Festival

On June 15th, the annual Brazilian Festival will take place (agin). There will be plenty of traditional music, dancing, and Brazilian food. Our festival is (allways) a good time. And if you miss this one, you won't get another chance until next year! Tickets are on sale (know.) Buy yours (todday)!

1. again **(2 points)**

2. always **(2)**

3. now **(2)**

4. today **(2)**

✏ **Write a Poem** Think about a tradition that's important to you. It can be one shared by a lot of people, or one that just your family shares. Then write a poem about the tradition. Use Spelling Words from the list. Responses will vary. **(2)**

Assessment Tip: Total **10** Points

Name _____

Rodeo Words

**Label each sentence True or False. If the
sentence is false, rewrite it to make it correct.**

1. A rodeo is a sporting event for cowboys.

   True **(2 points)**

   _____

2. Ceremonies are a set of acts that honor an event.

   True **(2)**

   _____

3. A celebrity is a person who is not very well-known.

   False. A celebrity is a famous person. **(2)**

   _____

4. An exhibition is a public show or display.

   True **(2)**

   _____

5. Experts are people who are beginners at an activity.

   False. Experts are people with much experience in an

   activity. **(2)**

6. Performers are people who watch a show.

   False. Performers are people who participate in a show.

   (2)

Name _____

Categories Chart

Answers will vary.

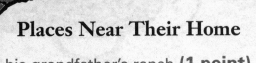

Places Near Their Home

his grandfather's ranch **(1 point)**

rocks with petroglyphs **(1)**

wall showing Yaqui Indian

    ceremonies **(1)**

grandparents' restaurant **(1)**

His Family

mother and father **(1)**

soon-to-be-born baby sister or

    brother **(1)**

grandparents **(1)**

cousins, aunts, and uncles **(1)**

Anthony Reynoso

Family Traditions

riding Mexican Rodeo style **(1)**

roping Mexican Rodeo style **(1)**

helping in grandparents' restaurant **(1)**

yearly family photo in traditional Mexican outfits **(1)**

celebrating birthdays together **(1)**

performing with father in public **(1)**

Assessment Tip: Total **14** Points

Name _____

Read All About It!

Answer the reporter's questions as if you were
Anthony Reynoso. Use complete sentences.
Answers may vary slightly. Examples are given.

1. What do you, your father, and your grandfather do on your grandfather's ranch?

   We rope and ride Mexican Rodeo style. **(2 points)**

   _____

2. Why do you practice roping so much?

   It takes years to learn roping; Dad and I perform at shows, and I don't want to

   mess up. **(2)**

3. Where do you and your dad often go on Saturdays and what do you do there?

   We often go to shows and exhibits to do roping together for tourists. **(2)**

   _____

4. What else do you do in your spare time?

   I look for petroglyphs, help at the family restaurant, go to grandfather's ranch,

   shoot baskets, collect basketball cards, and go to Slide Rock with the family. **(2)**

5. What special event are you looking forward to? Why?

   I am looking forward to being a brother to the new baby. I will teach the baby

   how to rope like me. **(2)**

Assessment Tip: Total **10** Points

Name _____

Family Categories

Read the story. Then complete the chart on the next page.

No Time to Spare

It's hard to find a good time to get in touch with my Aunt
Mickey Sobol. It's even harder to reach my cousins Karen and
Ike. That's because they're always busy.

Their day starts at sunup when Karen and Ike head for the
barn to feed their sheep. Meanwhile, Aunt Mickey does chores
and fixes the lunches. After breakfast, my cousins take the bus
to school, and Aunt Mickey leaves for work.

Each day, Aunt Mickey walks a mile to the little store she
runs by the lake. People from nearby vacation homes often
stop there, so she's always busy.

After school, Karen and Ike head for the animal shelter
down the road. Both of them want to be animal doctors,
so they like to help with the animals.

After dinner and homework, the family relaxes. Ike
usually reads, and Karen talks to a friend on the
computer. Aunt Mickey enjoys weaving colorful
blankets made of wool from their sheep.

Name _____

Family Categories

Write story details to complete this chart.

Answers may vary.

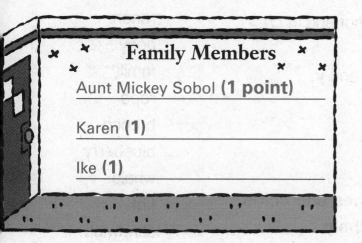

Family Members

Aunt Mickey Sobol **(1 point)**

Karen **(1)**

Ike **(1)**

Places Near Their Home

their barn

the store near the lake **(1)**

the vacation homes **(1)**

the animal shelter **(1)**

**The Sobol
Family**

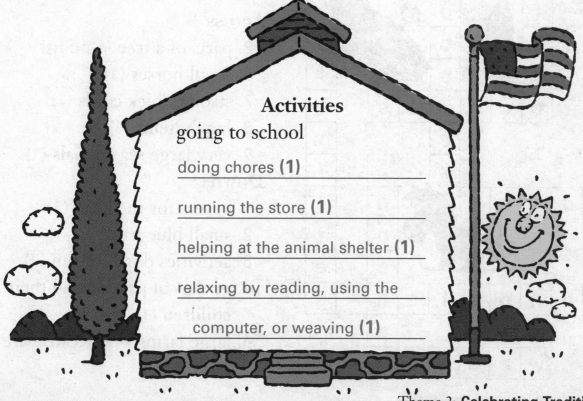

Activities

going to school

doing chores **(1)**

running the store **(1)**

helping at the animal shelter **(1)**

relaxing by reading, using the

computer, or weaving **(1)**

Name _____

Perfect Plurals

► Add *-s* to form the plural of most nouns.
  hat / hat**s**

► Add *-es* to form the plural of nouns that end in *ch*.
  lunch / lunch**es**

► When a noun ends with a consonant and *y*,
  change the *y* to *i* and add *-es*.
  penny / penn**ies**

Write the plural of the word that matches each clue in the puzzle. Use the Word Bank for help.

Across

2. parts of a tree **(1 point)**
5. small horses **(1)**
7. strong, thick cords **(1)**
8. lunch items **(1)**
9. very large sea animals **(1)**

Down

1. covers for the head **(1)**
2. small blue fruits **(1)**
3. activities done for fun **(1)**
4. groups of parents and their children **(1)**
6. large farms where cattle are raised **(1)**

Assessment Tip: Total **10** Points

Name _____

The Long *o* Sound

To spell a word with the /ō/ sound, remember that this sound can be spelled *oa*, *ow*, or *o*.

/ō/   oa, ow, o   c**oa**ch, bl**ow**, h**o**ld

► In the starred words *sew* and *though*, the /ō/ sound is spelled *ew* and *ough*.

Write each Spelling Word under its spelling of the /ō/ sound. Order of answers for each category may vary.

1. coach
2. blow
3. float
4. hold
5. sew*
6. though*
7. sold
8. soap
9. row
10. own
11. both
12. most

oa Spelling

coach **(1 point)**

float **(1)**

soap **(1)**

ow Spelling

blow **(1)**

row **(1)**

own **(1)**

o Spelling

hold **(1)**

sold **(1)**

both **(1)**

most **(1)**

Another Spelling

sew **(1)**

though **(1)**

Name _____

Spelling Spree

Word Maze Begin at the arrow and follow the
Word Maze to find seven Spelling Words. Write
the words in order.

1. coach
2. blow
3. float
4. hold
5. sew*
6. though*
7. sold
8. soap
9. row
10. own
11. both
12. most

1. blow **(1 point)**

2. though **(1)**

3. float **(1)**

4. hold **(1)**

5. row **(1)**

6. both **(1)**

7. sold **(1)**

Classifying Write the Spelling Word that
belongs in each group of words.

8. have, possess, own **(1)**

9. mend, stitch, sew **(1)**

10. teacher, trainer, coach **(1)**

11. toothpaste, shampoo, soap **(1)**

12. lots, many, most **(1)**

Assessment Tip: Total **12** Points

Name _____

Proofreading and Writing

Proofreading Circle the five misspelled Spelling Words in this poster. Then write each word correctly.

May 19, Sedona Fairgrounds
Roping Exhibition!

See (bothe) Reynoso roping champions!

Be ready to (holed) on to your hats! Thrill to the

tricks of Arizona's (moast) talented father and son

rope spinners. You won't believe your (oun) eyes!

Tickets will be (soled) at the gate.

Spelling Words

1. coach
2. blow
3. float
4. hold
5. sew*
6. though*
7. sold
8. soap
9. row
10. own
11. both
12. most

1. both **(2 Points)**

2. hold **(2)**

3. most **(2)**

4. own **(2)**

5. sold **(2)**

Write a Story About Yourself Have you ever worked hard to learn something? Maybe it was learning to swim, ride a bike, or even tie your shoes.

On a separate sheet of paper, write about a time when you worked very hard to learn something. Tell what the experience was like. Use Spelling Words from the list. Responses will vary. **(2)**

Word Sort

Parts of a Dictionary Read each word. Then alphabetize
the words and place each word with the correct guide words.

snore	lentil	outing
outfit	outgoing	lent
lesson	snowdrift	outlet
snow	leopard	snout

lengthy/let

lent **(1 point)** _____

lentil **(1)** _____

leopard **(1)** _____

lesson **(1)** _____

snip/snowdrop

snore **(1)** _____

snout **(1)** _____

snow **(1)** _____

snowdrift **(1)** _____

outfielder/outnumber

outfit **(1)** _____

outgoing **(1)** _____

outing **(1)** _____

outlet **(1)** _____

Name _____

Capital Letters

Capitalize each proper noun on the list below.

1. anthony reynoso <u>Anthony Reynoso **(1 point)**</u>

2. mexico <u>Mexico **(1)**</u>

3. tuesday <u>Tuesday **(1)**</u>

4. fifth avenue <u>Fifth Avenue **(1)**</u>

5. martha cooper <u>Martha Cooper **(1)**</u>

6. fourth of july <u>Fourth of July **(1)**</u>

7. united states of america <u>United States of America **(1)**</u>

8. *the keeping quilt* <u>The Keeping Quilt **(1)**</u>

9. mary ellen suarez <u>Mary Ellen Suarez **(1)**</u>

10. sedona, arizona <u>Sedona, Arizona **(1)**</u>

Write the proper noun or nouns in each sentence.

11. After school, Dad shows me a new rope trick. <u>Dad **(1)**</u>

12. On Saturday, we go to the Sedona Rodeo. <u>Saturday, Sedona Rodeo **(1)**</u>

13. I read the new book by Ginger Gordon. <u>Ginger Gordon **(1)**</u>

14. Her first book was *My Two Worlds*. <u>My Two Worlds **(1)**</u>

15. She is a teacher in New York City. <u>New York City **(1)**</u>

Name _____

Charting Capital Letters

**This chart shows common and proper nouns. Add one
more proper noun for each common noun in the chart.**

Answers will vary. Suggested answers are given.

	Common Noun	Proper Noun
people	author	Ginger Gordon Maurice Sendak **(1 point)**
	boy	Anthony Reynoso Greg Johnson **(1)**
	relative	Dad Uncle Ray **(1)**
places	country	Mexico Canada **(1)**
	state	Arizona New Mexico **(1)**
	city	Guadalupe Sedona **(1)**
	street	Elm Street
		Santa Monica Boulevard **(1)**
	school	Booker T. Washington Elementary School
		Public School 41 **(1)**
things	river	Rio Grande Mississippi River **(1)**
	month	September January **(1)**
	day	Wednesday Thursday **(1)**
	language	Spanish French **(1)**

Assessment Tip: Total **12** Points

Proper Nouns

Remember that titles and their abbreviations, when used with a person's name, begin with a capital letter. Use a capital letter for a person's initials. End abbreviated titles with a period.

Proofread the letter below. Find the proper nouns and titles that need capital letters. Look for abbreviations that need periods. Use the proofreading marks to show the correction. (1 point for each correction.**)**

Proofreading Marks	
Make a small letter:	Çity
Make a capital letter:	boston
Add a period:	Mr⊙

Mr. Jason Brown
326 cypress Lane
sedona, AZ 86336

Dear Jason,

  Hello from new mexico! I came here with my friend, mrs⊙

williams. We saw some amazing rope tricks at the rodeo. The

winner of the contest was sheriff paul ortega.

  After the rodeo, we saw some real animals at the santa fe

National Forest. Our tour guide was dr⊙ angela t⊙ carson.

  I can't wait to get home and show our pictures to all of you

in mrs⊙ walter's class.

        Bye for now,

        Martin

Name _____

A Character Sketch

**Use this page to help you plan a character sketch. Write
whom your character sketch will be about. Then write at least
two interesting details about what the person looks like, what
the person says and does, and how you feel about the person.
The details should help you to describe the person.**
Answers will vary.

My
Character

_____

_____

How the Person Looks

1. (2 points) _____

2. _____

3. _____

What the Person Does

1. (2) _____

2. _____

3. _____

What the Person Says

1. (2) _____

_____

2. _____

_____

3. _____

_____

My Feelings About the Person

1. (2) _____

2. _____

3. _____

**Write your character sketch on a separate sheet of paper.
Use the details above. (2)**

Name _____

Correcting Run-On Sentences

► Two or more sentences that run together
make a **run-on sentence**.

► Correct run-on sentences by making separate sentences.
Add sentence end marks and capital letters where they are needed.

Run-On Sentence:

My friend Patricia loves to dance, she studies ballet every Saturday.

Corrected Sentences:

My friend Patricia loves to dance. **S**he studies ballet every Saturday.

If the sentence is correct, write *Correct*. **If it is a run-on sentence,
write it as two sentences.**

1. My favorite singer is Gloria Estefan, she sings great songs.

My favorite singer is Gloria Estefan. She sings great songs. **(2 points)**

_____

2. My father runs a restaurant in town, he's the best cook in the world.

My father runs a restaurant in town. He's the best cook in the world. **(2)**

_____

3. My mother is a math teacher at Yorkstone High School.

Correct **(2)**

_____

4. My sister Tasha loves gymnastics, she does the best cartwheels.

My sister Tasha loves gymnastics. She does the best cartwheels. **(2)**

_____

Name _____

Word Search

**Write the letter of the correct definition next to each word.
Then find the words in the puzzle and circle them.**

1. wealth c **(1)**

2. royalty b **(1)**

3. collection e **(1)**

4. embroidered a **(1)**

5. symbols d **(1)**

6. flourish f **(1)**

a. decorated by sewing
b. kings and queens
c. lots of money or
   belongings
d. drawings that stand for
   something
e. a group of items with
   something in common
f. a showy waving motion

E	M	B	R	O	I	D	E	R	E	D	D	D
K	J	J	M	F	C	O	Q	W	H	R	G	N
O	L	U	J	Y	R	R	O	Y	A	L	T	Y
R	O	Q	I	P	C	C	O	S	H	T	C	A
X	S	L	D	E	E	O	W	V	E	O	J	N
F	P	X	C	C	O	L	L	E	C	T	O	R
H	L	J	J	M	F	L	O	U	R	I	S	H
L	V	I	M	G	C	E	U	U	N	N	J	B
N	E	F	W	I	M	C	P	W	W	D	J	S
S	S	W	E	A	L	T	H	L	P	Z	K	J
S	E	C	J	W	S	I	J	E	L	M	E	L
W	Y	S	Y	M	B	O	L	S	U	R	Q	W
N	T	R	J	B	V	N	D	Y	Y	S	X	O

Assessment Tip: Total **6** Points

Name ______________________________

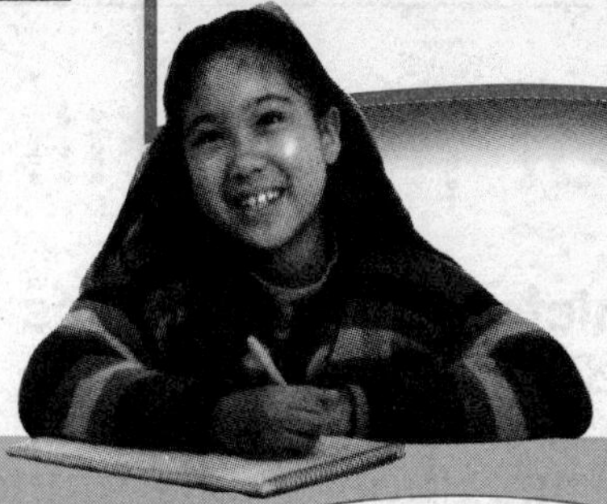

Cluster Maps

Answers may vary. Students may find more than four details about each topic given. Possible answers shown here; accept reasonable responses.

Aunt Phoebe

- a collector of life **(1 point)**
- "There's no place in her house to be bored." **(1)**
- "Daddy says she lives in a junk pile." **(1)**
- She tells Amber stories and gives her mocha to drink. **(1)**

adinkra cloth

- "It runs like a white river across the floor." **(1)**
- It's made by the Ashanti people. **(1)**
- "It's made of silk and feels smooth." **(1)**
- Only royalty used to wear it. **(1)**

Assessment Tip: Total **8** Points

Name _____

What the Cloth Says

Complete these sentences about *The Talking Cloth*.
Answers will vary.

Aunt Phoebe tells Amber about many things. Today they

talk about <u>adinkra cloth from Ghana/Africa. **(2 points)**</u> At one

time, only <u>royalty **(1)**</u> wore it.

Amber learns that the cloth talks because the colors and

symbols <u>send a message/mean something **(2)**</u>. If the cloth is

white, that means <u>joy **(1)**</u>. If it is blue,

that means <u>love **(1)**</u>. The symbols on it

stand for ideas like <u>faith/power **(1)**</u> and

<u>love **(1)**</u>.

Aunt Phoebe wraps the cloth around Amber. Now she

feels as if she's an <u>Ashanti princess **(1)**</u> with

<u>people who've also worn the cloth **(2)**</u> gathered

around her.

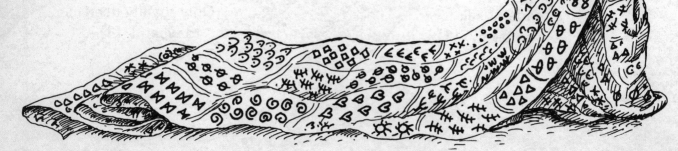

Name _____

Details for Playing

Read the story. Then complete the chart on the next page.

Not for Sale

As Zack walked along, he passed stores with window displays that didn't interest him. Then he came to a store window full of old, worn things. A strange object caught his eye. The wood was dark and shiny smooth. It was long, about as long as Zack's arm, and had six little bowls along each of its sides. At each end was a larger bowl, which made fourteen little bowls in all.

Curious, Zack went inside for a better look. Noting Zack's interest, the shopkeeper explained that the wooden object was a game board carved by an Ashanti artist in Ghana, Africa. The shopkeeper pulled up two chairs and told Zack to sit down. Then he scooped out some brown seeds from one of the bowls and showed Zack how to play *wari*, an Ashanti board game.

At least once a week Zack stopped by the shop to play *wari* with Mr. Oban, the shopkeeper. Both he and Mr. Oban enjoyed playing. And when they finished, Mr. Oban always put the game board away in the back room. It was no longer for sale.

Name _____

Details for Playing

continued

Complete this chart. List details from the story "Not for Sale." Answers may vary.

List of Details
the game board
1. It's made of dark, shiny wood with fourteen little bowls carved into it. **(1)**
2. It was carved by an Ashanti artist. **(1)**
3. It's used for a game called *wari*. **(1)**
4. It's no longer for sale. **(1)**
Zack's feelings
1. He's curious about the wooden object. **(1)**
2. He enjoys playing *wari*. **(1)**
Zack's actions
1. He notices the wooden object in the window. **(1)**
2. He goes inside for a better look. **(1)**
3. He learns how to play *wari*. **(1)**
4. He and Mr. Oban play the game often. **(1)**

Assessment Tip: Total **10** Points

Name _____

Shorten It!

A **contraction** is the short way of saying or writing two words. The apostrophe (') takes the place of one or more letters.

Fill in the spaces below to show how contractions are formed.

1. he   +   is   =   he's **(1 point)**

2. she   +   will   =   she'll **(1)**

3. was   +   not   =   wasn't **(1)**

4. they   +   are   =   they're **(1)**

5. I   +   will   =   I'll **(1)**

6. it **(1)**   +   is **(1)**   =   it's

7. you **(1)**   +   are **(1)**   =   you're

8. has **(1)**   +   not **(1)**   =   hasn't

9. is **(1)**   +   not **(1)**   =   isn't

10. we **(1)**   +   are **(1)**   =   we're

Name _____

Three-Letter Clusters

When two or more consonants with different sounds are written together, they form a **consonant cluster**. When you are spelling a word that has a consonant cluster, say the word aloud and listen for the different consonant sounds. Remember, some words begin with the consonant clusters *spr*, *str*, and *thr*.

spring   **str**ong   **thr**ow

Some other words have unexpected spelling patterns.

► A beginning /n/ sound may be spelled *kn*, as in **kn**ee. (The *k* is silent.)

► A beginning /r/ sound may be spelled *wr*, as in **wr**ap. (The *w* is silent.)

► A final /ch/ sound may be spelled *tch*, as in pa**tch**. (The *t* is silent.)

Spelling Words

1. spring
2. knee
3. throw
4. patch
5. strong
6. wrap
7. three
8. watch
9. street
10. know
11. spread
12. write

Write each Spelling Word under its proper category.
Order of answers for each category may vary.

Three-Letter Clusters	Unexpected Consonant Patterns
spring **(1 point)**	knee **(1)**
throw **(1)**	patch **(1)**
strong **(1)**	wrap **(1)**
three **(1)**	watch **(1)**
street **(1)**	know **(1)**
spread **(1)**	write **(1)**

Assessment Tip: Total **12** Points

Name _____

Spelling Spree

Hink Pinks **Write the Spelling Word that fits the clue and rhymes with the given word.**

Example: just-born twins   **new** _____ *two*

1. a ball tossed to a baby   **low** _____
2. jam or jelly   **bread** _____
3. cord for a kite on a day in May   _____ **string**
4. you and two friends on a school holiday   _____ **free**
5. a tidy block to live on   **neat** _____
6. plastic covering on a bottle top   **cap** _____

Spelling Words

1. spring
2. knee
3. throw
4. patch
5. strong
6. wrap
7. three
8. watch
9. street
10. know
11. spread
12. write

1. <u>throw **(1 point)**</u>   4. <u>three **(1)**</u>

2. <u>spread **(1)**</u>   5. <u>street **(1)**</u>

3. <u>spring **(1)**</u>   6. <u>wrap **(1)**</u>

Finding Words **Write the Spelling Words in each of these words.**

7. patchwork   <u>patch **(1)**</u>

8. headstrong   <u>strong **(1)**</u>

9. kneecap   <u>knee **(1)**</u>

10. wristwatch   <u>watch **(1)**</u>

11. knowing   <u>know **(1)**</u>

12. writer   <u>write **(1)**</u>

Name _____

Proofreading and Writing

Proofreading Circle the five misspelled Spelling
Words in this character sketch. Then write each
word correctly on the lines below.

Amber's aunt has been everywhere. Aunt

Phoebe takes a long trip to a faraway place every

(springe). She has been to Africa (thee) times. When

she visits a foreign country, she wants to (nowe) what it

is like to live there. Every time she walks down a new

street, she likes to (wache) the people carefully. She

notices how they dress and listens to how they speak.

Later, she always takes the time to (rite) to Amber

about her experiences. I admire Aunt Phoebe because

she is always learning something new.

1. spring **(2 points)**	4.	watch **(2)**
2. three **(2)**	5.	write **(2)**
3. know **(2)**		

Spelling Words

1. spring
2. knee
3. throw
4. patch
5. strong
6. wrap
7. three
8. watch
9. street
10. know
11. spread
12. write

Write a Thank-You Note Has a relative or friend ever given
you a special or unusual gift? What was it that made it special?
**On a separate sheet of paper, write a thank-you note for the
gift. Make sure to tell the person you are thanking why the gift
is special to you. Use Spelling Words from the list.** Responses will vary. **(2)**

Name _____

Rhyming Crossword

Complete the crossword puzzle by writing the correct rhyme for each word. Remember that a rhyming word has the same end sound as another word. Choose your answers from the words in the box.

Vocabulary

trip
map
lace
cause
wealth
silk
smiles
sled
smells
might

Across

2. Object used to go across snow. Rhymes with *said*. **(1 point)**
3. A happy person does this. Rhymes with *miles*. **(1)**
7. A piece of string used to tie a shoe. Rhymes with *face*. **(1)**
8. Riches. Rhymes with *health*. **(1)**
9. A voyage. Rhymes with *lip*. **(1)**
10. Drawings of the earth's surface. Rhymes with *traps*. **(1)**

Down

1. What your nose does. Rhymes with *tells*. **(1)**
4. Strength. Rhymes with *right*. **(1)**
5. A smooth, shiny fabric. Rhymes with *milk*. **(1)**
6. A reason. Rhymes with *pause*. **(1)**

Name _____

Circling Nouns

Circle each singular common noun in the sentences below.
Underline each plural common noun.

1. Aunt Phoebe collects many <u>things</u>. **(1 point)**

2. The (cloth) is embroidered in <u>sections</u>. **(1)**

3. The (fabric) has no <u>patches</u>. **(1)**

4. The <u>patterns</u> show many <u>colors</u> and <u>shapes</u>. **(1)**

5. Phoebe gave her (niece) two <u>boxes</u>. **(1)**

6. Inside, she found two colorful <u>dresses</u>. **(1)**

Write each plural noun in the correct column below.

Add -*s* to form the plural	Add -*es* to form the plural
things **(1 point)**	patches **(1)**
sections **(1)**	boxes **(1)**
patterns **(1)**	dresses **(1)**
colors **(1)**	
shapes **(1)**	

Assessment Tip: Total **14** Points

Name _____

Puzzling Plurals

Complete the puzzle by writing the plural of each noun.
Each noun is used only once. Some letters are filled in
to help you get started. (2 points for each answer)

Across		Down	
princess	princesses	symbol	symbols
basket	baskets	box	boxes
number	numbers	word	words
thing	things	pattern	patterns
tale	tales	dress	dresses

b a s k e t s

o   y

x   w   m

t a l e s   o   b

s   d   r   o

    r   d   l

p r i n c e s s e s

        s

a   t h i n g s   s

t   e

t   s

e

r

n u m b e r s

s

Name _____

Using Exact Nouns

**Write a noun that is more exact than each
general noun below.** Answers will vary.
Possible answers given.

1. animal   wolf **(1 point)**

2. tree   elm **(1)**

3. food   apple pie **(1)**

4. container   basket **(1)**

5. group   family **(1)**

**Read each sentence below. Then rewrite the sentence
on the line, substituting an exact noun for the general
noun or word in parentheses.**

6. Amber visited her favorite (person).

   Amber visited her favorite aunt. **(1)**

7. They shared a hot (drink) together.

   They shared a hot mocha together. **(1)**

8. Phoebe showed Amber a (thing).

   Phoebe showed Amber a cloth. **(1)**

9. The (thing) was covered with many (shapes).

   The cloth was covered with many symbols. **(1)**

10. One (shape) looked like a spinning (circle).

   One symbol looked like a spinning wheel. **(1)**

Assessment Tip: Total **10** Points

Name _____

Writing an Answer to a Question

When you write an answer to a question, follow these guidelines.

▶ Read the question carefully.

▶ Look for key words to help you decide what information the question is asking for.

▶ Give facts and examples that provide the information asked for.

For each question, write your answer on the lines. Write the start of the answer on the first answer line. Write the rest of the answer on the other answer lines. Answers will vary.

1. **Question:** What holiday do you enjoy most? Explain why.
   Turn the question into a statement. (2 points)

   _____

   Give facts that answer the question.

   (2) _____

   _____

2. **Question:** What place would you like to visit most? Explain why.
   Turn the question into a statement.

   (2) _____

   Give facts that answer the question.

   (2) _____

   _____

Writing Complete Sentences

A complete sentence contains both a naming part
and an action part.

Naming Part	Action Part
Aunt Phoebe	bought the adinkra cloth in Africa.

A sentence fragment is an incomplete sentence that has
just one sentence part.

Fragment (naming part only) The Ashanti people.
Fragment (action part only) Made adinkra cloths.

A complete sentence begins with a capital letter and ends
with the correct end punctuation.

Read each item. Write *Complete Sentence* **if the sentence
has both a naming part and an action part. If the item is a
sentence fragment, make it a complete sentence by adding
words. Write your complete sentence correctly.**

1. Means gold or riches. Possible answer: A yellow cloth means
   gold or riches. **(2 points)**

2. Amber and her father. Possible answer: Amber and her father visit
   Aunt Phoebe. **(2)**

3. Aunt Phoebe tells stories to Amber. Complete Sentence **(2)**

4. Drinks hot mocha. Possible answer: The young girl drinks hot mocha. **(2)**

Name _____

What Do You Think?

Answer the questions below. Use your glossary if you need help. Answers will vary.

1. Who are some of your ancestors? Where did they live?
(**2 points**) _____

_____

2. What could someone do to honor his or her
parents or family members?
(**2**) _____

_____

3. What is something you have learned by imitating another
person?
(**2**) _____

_____

4. What can you do to show respect for your teacher?
(**2**) _____

_____

5. How should young people act toward their elders?
(**2**) _____

_____

Name _____

Cluster Diagram

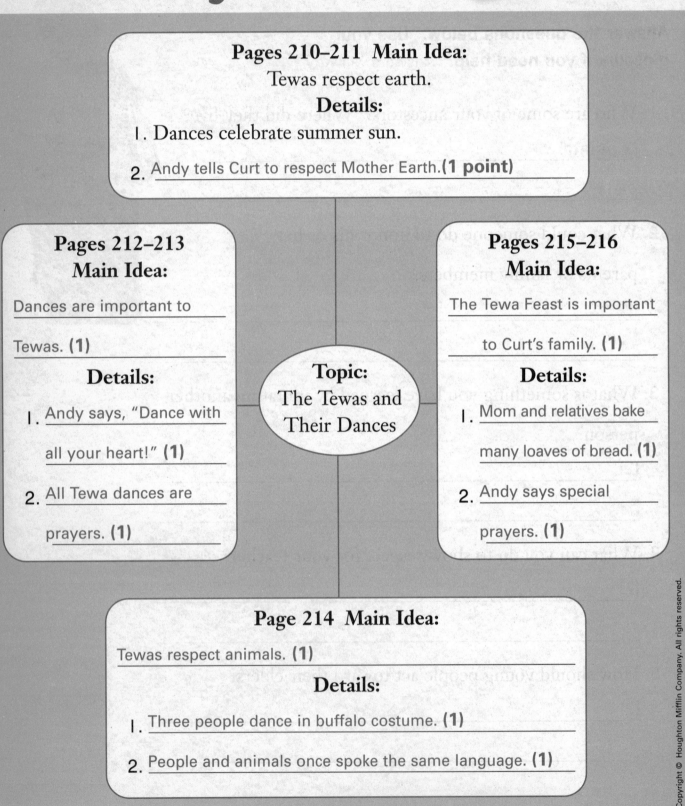

Pages 210–211 Main Idea:
Tewas respect earth.
Details:
1. Dances celebrate summer sun.
2. Andy tells Curt to respect Mother Earth.**(1 point)**

**Pages 212–213
Main Idea:**
Dances are important to
Tewas. **(1)**
Details:
1. Andy says, "Dance with
all your heart!" **(1)**
2. All Tewa dances are
prayers. **(1)**

Topic:
The Tewas and
Their Dances

**Pages 215–216
Main Idea:**
The Tewa Feast is important
to Curt's family. **(1)**
Details:
1. Mom and relatives bake
many loaves of bread. **(1)**
2. Andy says special
prayers. **(1)**

Page 214 Main Idea:
Tewas respect animals. **(1)**
Details:
1. Three people dance in buffalo costume. **(1)**
2. People and animals once spoke the same language. **(1)**

Assessment Tip: Total **10** Points

Name _____

Feast Day Questions

Answer each question about *Dancing Rainbows*.
Use complete sentences. Answers may vary somewhat.
Examples are given.

1. What is Feast Day?

   It is the day the Tewas in San Juan Pueblo, New Mexico, hold a big party to

   honor their patron saint and celebrate the power of the summer sun. **(2 points)**

2. Why do Curt, Andy, and the other Tewa people dance on Feast Day?

   They dance prayers to cure the sick, give thanks, bring the tribe together,

   ask for good crops, have fun, and bring rain. **(2)**

3. What sounds might you hear on Feast Day in the plaza?

   You might hear the sound of drums and bells, the shuffling of the dancers'

   feet, and singing in Tewa. **(2)**

4. When the Tewas dance, what might you see?

   Dancers of all ages dance many dances, including the Buffalo, Eagle, and

   Comanche Dances. They paint their faces and wear colorful costumes and

   headdresses. **(2)**

5. What did Andy do for his grandson and other young Tewas?

   He started a Tewa dance group for them where they learn traditional

   dances so they can dance at fairs, powwows, and other shows. **(2)**

Name _____

Mainly Ideas

Read the article. Then complete the diagram on the next page.

All About Eagles

How many different kinds of eagles do you think live in the world? If you guessed about sixty, you'd be right. Some kinds of eagles are large and some are small. Most are strong for their size. Some are even strong enough to lift food weighing almost as much as they do!

Eagles have been used as symbols of power and freedom. Some people call them the "king of birds" because of their strength and brave, proud looks. In 1782, the United States of America chose the bald eagle as its national bird.

Bald eagles are among the larger eagles. They can weigh anywhere from eight to thirteen pounds. These great birds can have wings that spread as much as seven feet across! Their heads are covered with white feathers, making them look "bald" from a distance.

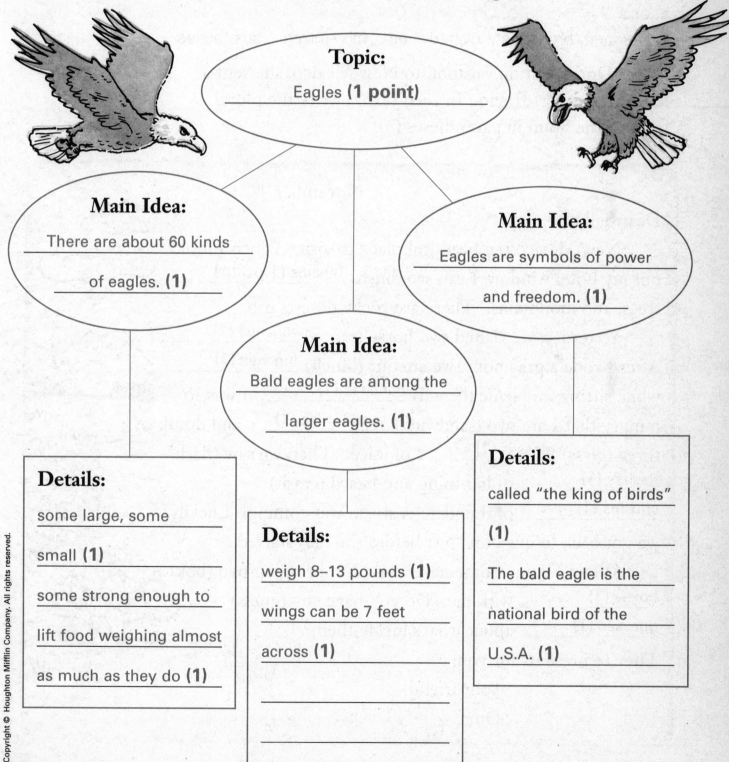

Name _____

Mainly Ideas continued

Complete the diagram with facts from "All About Eagles."

Topic:

Eagles **(1 point)**

Main Idea:

There are about 60 kinds

of eagles. **(1)**

Main Idea:

Eagles are symbols of power

and freedom. **(1)**

Main Idea:

Bald eagles are among the

larger eagles. **(1)**

Details:

some large, some

small **(1)**

some strong enough to

lift food weighing almost

as much as they do **(1)**

Details:

weigh 8–13 pounds **(1)**

wings can be 7 feet

across **(1)**

Details:

called "the king of birds"

(1)

The bald eagle is the

national bird of the

U.S.A. **(1)**

Dancing Rainbows

Structural Analysis
Plurals of Words Ending in
ch, sh, x, s

Name _____

More and More Plurals

Add -*es* to form the plural of a singular noun that ends in *ch*, *sh*, *x*, or *s*.

  branch/branch**es**   dish/dish**es**   mix/mix**es**   bus/bus**es**

When Dora went on vacation to New Mexico, she sent a letter to her best friend. In each blank, write the plural form of the noun in parentheses ( ).

November 4

Dear Sally,

   New Mexico is a beautiful place to visit. When I look out my hotel window, I can see (bush) <u>bushes **(1 point)**</u>, trees, and mountains. There are rocky deserts too.

   Yesterday, we visited two horse (ranch) <u>ranches **(1)**</u>. After I rode a gray pony, we ate our (lunch) <u>lunches **(1)**</u> while sitting on picnic (bench) <u>benches **(1)**</u>. I was so hungry that I ate two (sandwich) <u>sandwiches **(1)**</u> and drank three (glass) <u>glasses **(1)**</u> of juice! Then we saw (flash) <u>flashes **(1)**</u> of lightning and heard (crash) <u>crashes **(1)**</u> of thunder. A storm was coming! Luckily, we got back to our hotel just before the rain started.

   When I come home next week, I'm bringing two (box) <u>boxes **(1)**</u> with me. Do you have any (guess) <u>guesses **(1)**</u> about what's inside them?

They're presents for you!

                Your friend,

                Dora

Assessment Tip: Total **10** Points

Name _____

The Long *i* Sound

When you hear the /ī/ sound, think of the patterns *igh*, *i*, and *ie*.

/ī/ br**igh**t, w**i**ld, d**ie**

Write each Spelling Word under its spelling of the /ī/ sound. Order of answers for each category may vary.

Spelling Words

1. wild
2. bright
3. die
4. sight
5. child
6. pie
7. fight
8. lie
9. tight
10. tie
11. might
12. mind

igh Spelling

bright **(1 point)** _____

sight **(1)** _____

fight **(1)** _____

tight **(1)** _____

might **(1)** _____

ie Spelling

die **(1)** _____

pie **(1)** _____

lie **(1)** _____

tie **(1)** _____

i Spelling

wild **(1)** _____

child **(1)** _____

mind **(1)** _____

Name _____

Spelling Spree

Sentence Pairs Write the Spelling Word that best completes each pair of sentences.

Example: A jet does not fly low. It flies *high* .

1. These shoes are not loose. They are _____.
2. My sister is not a grownup. She is a _____.
3. A tiger is not tame. It is _____.
4. I will not have cake for dessert. I will have _____.
5. Neither team won. The score was a _____.
6. The sunshine is not dim today. It is _____.
7. He did not tell the truth. He told a _____.

1. tight **(1 point)**   5. tie **(1)**

2. child **(1)**   6. bright **(1)**

3. wild **(1)**   7. lie **(1)**

4. pie **(1)**

Missing Letters Each missing letter fits in ABC order between the other two letters. Write the missing letters to spell a Spelling Word.

Example: e _ g h _ j m _ o c _ e *find*

8. c _ e h _ j d _ f   8. die **(1)**

9. l _ n h _ j m _ o c _ e   9. mind **(1)**

10. e _ g h _ j f _ h g _ i s _ u   10. fight **(1)**

Assessment Tip: Total **10** Points

Name _____

Definition Derby

Read the dictionary entry for the word *dance.* **Then write sample sentences as directed.** Answers will vary.

dance (dăns) *verb* **1.** To move with rhythmic steps and motions, usually in time to music. **2.** To move lightly and quickly: *The waves danced in the moonlight.*

◇ *noun* **1.** A set of rhyme steps or motions, usually done in time to music. **2.** A gathering at which people dance. **3.** The art of dancing.

dance (dăns) ◇ *verb* **danced, dancing** ◇ *noun, plural* **dances**

1. Write a sentence using the most common meaning of *dance.*

   (2 points) _____

2. Write a sentence using noun definition number 3.

   (2) _____

3. Write a sentence using noun definition number 1.

   (2) _____

4. Write a sentence using verb definition number 2.

   (2) _____

5. Write a sentence using the least common meaning of *dance.*

   (2) _____

120   Theme 2: **Celebrating Traditions**
Assessment Tip: Total **10** Points

Name _____

Proofreading and Writing

Proofreading Circle the five misspelled Spelling Words in this page from a travel brochure. Then write each word correctly.

Spelling Words

1. wild
2. bright
3. die
4. sight
5. child
6. pie
7. fight
8. lie
9. tight
10. tie
11. might
12. mind

> ### Visit Beautiful New Mexico!
>
> Come to New Mexico and discover a land of amazing beauty! Explore wonderful deserts bathed in (brit) sunshine. Hike in our mountains and experience adventure in the (wilde!) Relax your (minde) and body at one of our many resorts. Enjoy the (siet) of colorful hot-air balloons in Albuquerque. Spend a week with us, and you just (mieght) never go home again! That's no lie.

1. bright **(2 points)**
2. wild **(2)**
3. mind **(2)**
4. sight **(2)**
5. might **(2)**

Write an Explanation The Tewas believe that the eagle is a special animal that carries messages to earth. If you could wear an animal costume, what animal would you choose to be?

On a separate sheet of paper, tell what animal you would choose and explain why you think this animal is special. Use Spelling Words from the list. Responses will vary. **(2)**

Name _____

Beat the Drum for Plurals

Circle all the plural nouns and write each one in the correctly labeled drum.

1. The Tewa (children) practice dancing.
2. (Men) and (women) prepare for a festival.
3. The (skies) are clear and blue.
4. (Families) arrive from many different (cities).
5. The (parties) are about to begin.
6. (Loaves) of bread are stacked on the table.
7. (People) stomp their (feet).
8. Sweet (candies) are a special treat.

Change *y* to *i* and add *-es*

skies **(2 points)**

families **(2)**

cities **(2)**

parties **(2)**

candies **(2)**

Special Plural Forms

children **(2)**

men **(2)**

women **(2)**

loaves **(2)**

people **(2)**

feet **(2)**

Name _____

Completing with Plurals

Complete the story by writing the plural form for each noun in parentheses.

1. The ___skies (2 points)___ are sunny and clear. (sky)

2. All the relatives help bake many ___loaves (2)___ of bread for the feast. (loaf)

3. Many ___families (2)___ have come to the celebration. (family)

4. At last, six ___men (2)___ begin to dance. (man)

5. Their ___feet (2)___ fly above the ground. (foot)

Assessment Tip: Total **10** Points

Proofreading for Noun Endings

Name _____

Proofread the paragraphs below. Find plurals of nouns that are spelled incorrectly. Circle each misspelled plural. Then write each correctly spelled noun on the lines below. Use a dictionary for help.

> After sunrise, the Tewa (mens) and (womens) gather. Mothers carry their smiling (babys). (Fatheres) walk with their sons and daughters. People arrive from many (citys). They look forward to the dances and the (storys).
>
> Three (childs) wear buffalo (costumies). They are dancers. Their feet move in beautiful (patternes). After the dance, everyone feasts on (loafs) of bread and tasty treats.

Regular	Ends in consonant + *y*	Special plurals
fathers **(1 point)**	babies **(1)**	men **(1)**
costumes **(1)**	cities **(1)**	women **(1)**
patterns **(1)**	stories **(1)**	children **(1)**
		loaves **(1)**

Name _____

Writing a News Article

Use this page to plan and organize your news article about a holiday or celebration. When you finish, use the outline to write your article on a separate sheet of paper.

1. Holiday or Celebration _____

   (1 point) _____

2. Who? _____

   (1) _____

3. What? _____

   (1) _____

4. When? _____

   (1) _____

5. Where? _____

   (1) _____

6. Why? _____

   (1) _____

7. How? _____

   (1) _____

8. Interesting Opening Sentence _____

   (2) _____

9. Interesting Headline **(1)** _____

Assessment Tip: Total **10** Points

Name _____

Newspaper Article

Audience A good newspaper article includes details that help
the audience picture what they did not witness themselves.

**Read the newspaper article. Then answer each question
based on some facts or details from the article.**

> In the past month, San Juan Pueblo has had no rain. The
> elders of the Tewa tribe who live there have decided to hold a
> rain dance. The dancing will begin at nine in the morning and
> last until noon. The purpose of the dance is to ask the Tewa
> ancestors to bring rain. Andy Garcia is an elder of the tribe.
> He says that the Tewa believe that their ancestors come back as
> raindrops to water their crops and give them water to drink.

1. Who are the Tewa?

   Answers may vary. The Tewa are a tribe of Native Americans. **(2 points)**

2. Where will the rain dance be held?

   Answers may vary. The rain dance will be held at San Juan Pueblo. **(2)**

3. What would make an interesting beginning to the article?

   Answers will vary. **(3)**

   _____

   _____

4. What would make an interesting headline for this article?

   Answers will vary. **(3)**

**Congratulations! You are a good reporter! Now write your new,
improved article on a separate piece of paper.**

Name _____

Filling in the Blank

Use the test-taking strategies and tips you have learned to help you complete fill-in-the-blank items about *The Keeping Quilt*. This practice will help you when you take this kind of test.

Read each item. At the bottom of the page, fill in the circle for the answer that best completes the sentence.

1   By pointing out that Anna was speaking English in only six months while her parents never learned much of it, the author shows that —

   Ⓐ Anna was smarter than her parents

   Ⓑ it is easier for young people to learn a new language

   Ⓒ it is important for children to go to school

   Ⓓ Anna's parents wanted to move back to Russia

2   The author probably believes that it is important to remember your homeland, because in the story she has —

   Ⓕ Anna's parents speak Russian rather than English

   Ⓖ the neighborhood ladies cut out animals and flowers for the quilt

   Ⓗ a detailed description of Anna's home in Russia

   Ⓙ Anna want a quilt to remind the family of Russia

ANSWER ROWS   I Ⓐ ● Ⓒ Ⓓ (5 points)   2 Ⓕ Ⓖ Ⓗ ● (5)

Name _____

Filling in the Blank continued

3 The quilt is not always mentioned in the story, but the author lets the reader know how special it is to Anna by having pictures that show —

(A) the quilt at important events in Anna's life

(B) Anna giving it to her husband as a gift

(C) the quilt as the background in every scene

(D) how Anna makes it into something new and different as she gets older

4 The author has Mary Ellen tell her daughter about the pieces of cloth that went into making the quilt to —

(F) encourage Patricia to make her own quilt

(G) describe how the quilt was made

(H) teach Patricia about her family

(J) explain to Patricia how to recycle old clothes

5 The author ends the story by saying "Traci and Steven were now all grownup and getting ready to start their own lives," so the reader knows that —

(A) the family doesn't need the quilt anymore

(B) the quilt will continue to be used

(C) the author plans to write another book about the quilt

(D) the quilt is too old and worn out for Traci and Steven

ANSWER ROWS   3 Ⓐ Ⓑ Ⓒ ⬤ (5)   5 Ⓐ ⬤ Ⓒ Ⓓ (5)
　　　　　　　4 Ⓕ Ⓖ ⬤ Ⓙ (5)

Assessment Tip: Total **25** Points

Name _____

Spelling Review

Write Spelling Words from the list to answer the questions. Order of answers in each category may vary.

1–9. Which nine words have the long *a* or long *e* sound?

1. lay **(1 point)**

2. feel **(1)**

3. seem **(1)**

4. three **(1)**

5. speak **(1)**

6. need **(1)**

7. leave **(1)**

8. paint **(1)**

9. street **(1)**

10–16. Which seven words have the long *o* sound?

10. hold **(1)**

11. own **(1)**

12. most **(1)**

13. float **(1)**

14. row **(1)**

15. both **(1)**

16. know **(1)**

17–22. Which six words have the long *i* sound?

17. wild **(1)**

18. might **(1)**

19. lie **(1)**

20. mind **(1)**

21. bright **(1)**

22. tie **(1)**

23–25. Which three words end with these letters?

23. _____tch   24. _____ead   25. _____ap

23. patch **(1)**

24. spread **(1)**

25. wrap **(1)**

Spelling Words

1. lay
2. feel
3. hold
4. wild
5. might
6. paint
7. seem
8. patch
9. three
10. own
11. speak
12. need
13. lie
14. most
15. spread
16. float
17. row
18. leave
19. both
20. wrap
21. know
22. mind
23. street
24. bright
25. tie

Assessment Tip: Total **25** Points

Name _____

Spelling Spree

Rhyme Time **Write the Spelling Word that rhymes with the word in dark print.**

Example: A plump kitty is a _____fat_____ **cat.**

1. A nice brain is a **kind** __mind **(1 point)**__.

2. An animal life jacket is a **goat** __float **(1)**__.

3. An unreal piece of clothing is a __tie **(1)**__ **lie.**

4. Baby triplets are a **wee** __three **(1)**__.

1. paint
2. leave
3. might
4. need
5. mind
6. tie
7. spread
8. float
9. three
10. wild
11. patch
12. street

Word Search **Underline the eight hidden Spelling Words. Then write the words.**

Example: abe<u>needle</u>an ____needle____

5. reda<u>wild</u>ell

6. y<u>might</u>aledfl

7. enr<u>street</u>alp

8. knp<u>aint</u>ilke

9. terilo<u>need</u>um

10. grp<u>atch</u>ibror

11. olgera<u>spread</u>

12. wril<u>leave</u>kn

5. __wild **(1)**__

6. __might **(1)**__

7. __street **(1)**__

8. __paint **(1)**__

9. __need **(1)**__

10. __patch **(1)**__

11. __spread **(1)**__

12. __leave **(1)**__

Assessment Tip: Total **12** Points

Proofreading and Writing

Proofreading **Circle the six misspelled Spelling
Words in this play. Then write each word correctly.**

Spelling Words

1. lay
2. most
3. wrap
4. lie
5. feel
6. seem
7. hold
8. speak
9. own
10. bright
11. row
12. both
13. know
14. mind

Grandpa: Let's (rapp) the gifts in (brite) yellow paper.

Joe: We can (laye) it on the table for Mom.

Grandpa: Be careful how you (hoald) it.

Joe: You (kno) we (bouth) did a good job!

1. wrap **(1)**   3. lay **(1)**   5. know **(1)**

2. bright **(1)**   4. hold **(1)**   6. both **(1)**

Complete a Letter **Use Spelling Words to complete
the following letter.**

Thanksgiving makes me 7. feel **(1)** very
happy. Our family has its 8. own **(1)** traditions.
My grandfather will 9. speak **(1)** his 10. mind **(1)**
about sharing with others. A feast will 11. lie **(1)**
on the table, with many plates in a 12. row **(1)** .
The 13. most **(1)** simple dishes 14. seem **(1)**
even tastier then.

Write a Description **On a separate sheet of paper,
describe a celebration you enjoy. Use the Spelling Words.**
Responses will vary. **(2)**

Name _____

It's Tricky!

Compare the three trickster tales. Answers will vary.

► Draw a cover cartoon for each tale.
► Write enough about the story to make someone want to read it.

For example:
Rabbit races Turtle.
But in the end, Turtle wins!
How does slow Turtle beat
   fast Rabbit?

Aunt Fox and the Fried Fish

(4 points) _____

_____

_____

Hungry Spider

(4) _____

_____

_____

Rabbit Races with Turtle

(4) _____

_____

_____

Name _____

What Makes a Trickster Tale?

After reading each selection, complete the chart below to tell why each story is a trickster tale.

	Name the tricksters	Who was tricked?	What was the trick?
Hungry Spider	Spider, Turtle (**1 point**)	Turtle, then Spider (**1**)	Making Turtle wash his feet; making Spider eat underwater without weights (**2**)
Rabbit Races with Turtle	Turtle (**1**)	Rabbit (**1**)	A different turtle climbed over each ridge. (**2**)
Aunt Fox and the Fried Fish	Aunt Fox (**1**)	Uncle Fox, Uncle Tiger (**1**)	Making Uncle Tiger and Uncle Fox believe two different, untrue stories about each other (**2**)

Assessment Tip: Total **12** Points

Name _____

Incredible Stories

What do you think makes a story incredible? Is it the characters, the setting, or the events? Complete the web with words or phrases that describe an incredible story.

(2 points)

(2)

(2)

Incredible
Stories

(2)

(2)

Now list some books, movies, or real events that you think are incredible. (5)

_____

_____

_____

_____

Name _____

Incredible Stories

Fill in the chart as you read the stories. Sample answers shown.

	What incredible thing happens?	How do the characters respond?
Dogzilla	A dog comes out of a volcano and scares a city full of mice. **(2 points)**	The mice give Dogzilla a bath. **(3)**
The Mysterious Giant of Barletta	A statue comes alive to help a town. **(2)**	The giant and the townspeople work together to trick the army. **(3)**
Raising Dragons	A dragon hatches out of an egg and is raised by a little girl. **(2)**	The little girl takes Hank to Dragon Island and comes back with more dragon eggs. **(3)**
The Garden of Abdul Gasazi	A magician turns a dog into a duck. **(2)**	Alan decides he won't be tricked again, but Miss Hester can't explain how Alan's hat got back on her porch. **(3)**

Assessment Tip: Total **20** Points

Name _____

Monster Words

Circle the two words that are most alike in meaning.

1. (colossal)
   small
   (big) (1 point)

2. (animal)
   (creature)
   tree (1)

3. strong
   (brave)
   (heroic) (1)

4. (huge)
   (monstrous)
   bad (1)

5. enormous
   (terrifying)
   (scary) (1)

6. (tremendous)
   tiny
   (large) (1)

7. (frightening)
   fun
   (horrifying) (1)

8. little
   (tremendous)
   (colossal) (1)

9. (terrifying)
   (horrifying)
   monstrous (1)

10. (colossal)
    heroic
    (monstrous) (1)

Name _____

Fantasy and Realism Chart

Sample answers provided.

Story Events and Characters	Fantasy (Make Believe)	Realism (True-to-Life)
	1. A city is built and run by mice **(1 point)** .	1. The wind carries the scent of barbecue sauce into the distance. **(1)**
	2. A monster dog attacks the mouse city. **(1)**	2. A real dog can cause trouble. **(1)**
	3. Mice send out an army. **(1)**	3. Cities have emergency meetings and emergency help, such as police officers and fire fighters. **(1)**
	4. Mice have an emergency meeting. **(1)**	4. Dogs often hate baths. **(1)**
	5. The mice chase off Dogzilla with a bath. **(1)**	5. Dogs have puppies. **(1)**

Assessment Tip: Total **10** Points

Name _____

Fix the Facts

Read this newspaper story about *Dogzilla*, and draw a line through the mistakes. Then write what really happened. Sample paragraph provided.

Monster Makes News!

The ~~people~~ in Mousopolis took part in a Cook-Off. It was ~~winter~~, and smoke lifted over the city. Soon a strange sound was heard: "~~Quack . . . quack~~." Then Dogzilla climbed out of a ~~cave~~!

The troops were sent out. But Dogzilla ~~hid~~, and the troops ~~danced~~ home. Dogzilla wandered the city ~~looking for a place to sleep~~. The mice called a meeting. The mice decided the only way to defeat Dogzilla was to think like a ~~donkey~~. So they ~~munched grass and waited~~. It worked! Dogzilla ran out of town. And the problem was solved ~~forever~~.

The **mice (1 point)** in Mousopolis took part in a Cook-off. It was **summer, (1)** and smoke lifted over the city. Soon a strange sound was heard: **"Sniff. . . sniff." (1)** Then Dogzilla climbed out of a **volcano. (1)**

The troops were sent out. But Dogzilla **breathed on the mice (1)** and the troops **ran** home. **(1)** Dogzilla wandered the city **doing a lot of damage. (1)** The mice called a meeting. The mice decided the only way to defeat Dogzilla was to think like a **dog. (1)** So they **gave Dogzilla a bath. (1)** It worked! Dogzilla ran out of town. And the problem was solved **until the Second Annual Barbecue Cook-Off. (1)**

Name _____

A Real Fantasy

**Read the story. Find parts that are fantasy
and parts that could happen in real life.**

A Fish Tale

Way up north, it's cold and dark for much of the year.
But that's how polar bears like it, or at least, that's what
people think.

"I hate the cold and dark," said Ursa Bear from her seat by
the fire. "I want to go where it's warm!"

"That's silly!" snapped her sister. "Now go catch some
fish for dinner."

Soon Ursa sat by the ocean's edge, waiting. Her first catch
was a mackerel with shiny scales.

"Please don't eat me," begged the fish. "If you let me go,
I'll grant you one wish!"

"Can you do that?" asked Ursa. "Then I wish I were
somewhere sunny and warm! Here, my friend, I'll let you go."

At once Ursa found herself on a sunny beach next to some
surprised people. "This is great!" she cried. "Now where can I
find a beach chair?"

The mackerel was even happier. "That's the tenth bear
I've wished away today!" he laughed. "Soon my fish friends
and I will be all by ourselves."

A Real Fantasy continued

Finish the chart. List five fantasy details and five realistic details from the story.

Fantasy Details (make-believe)	Realistic Details (true-to-life)
1. polar bears who talk **(1 point)**	1. polar bears living in the far north **(1)**
2. polar bears wishing to be in a warm place **(1)**	2. cold and dark way up north **(1)**
3. a talking fish **(1)**	3. bears catching and eating fish **(1)**
4. a fish who grants wishes **(1)**	4. mackerel with shiny scales **(1)**
5. a polar bear who wants a beach chair **(1)**	5. people on a warm, sunny beach **(1)**

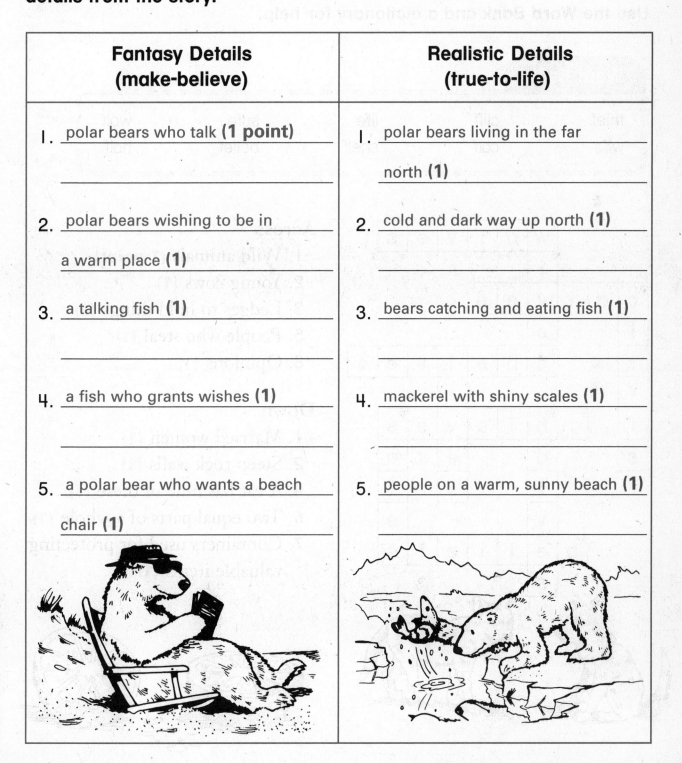

Plurals Puzzle

Write the plural noun that matches each clue in the puzzle.
Use the Word Bank and a dictionary for help.

Word Bank

| thief | cliff | life | safe | wolf |
| wife | calf | shelf | belief | half |

Across

1. Wild animals **(1 point)**
2. Young cows **(1)**
3. Ledges to hold things **(1)**
5. People who steal **(1)**
8. Opinions **(1)**

Down

1. Married women **(1)**
2. Steep rock walls **(1)**
4. A cat has nine of these **(1)**
6. Two equal parts of a whole **(1)**
7. Containers used for protecting valuable items **(1)**

Assessment Tip: Total **10** Points

Name _____

The Vowel Sounds in *clown* and *lawn*

The /ou/ sound you hear in *clown* can be spelled with the pattern *ow* or *ou*. The /ô/ sound you hear in *lawn* can be spelled with these patterns: *aw*, *o*, or *a* before *l*.

/ou/ **cl**ow**n**, s**ou**nd

/ô/ **law**n, cl**o**th, t**a**lk

▶ In the starred word *would*, *ou* does not spell the /ou/ sound. Instead, *ou* spells the vowel sound you hear in the word *book*.

Write each Spelling Word under its vowel sound.

Order of answers for each category may vary.

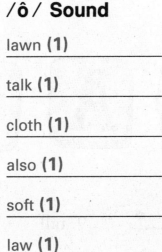

Spelling Words

1. clown
2. lawn
3. talk
4. sound
5. cloth
6. would*
7. also
8. mouth
9. crown
10. soft
11. count
12. law

/ou/ Sound

clown **(1 point)**

sound **(1)**

mouth **(1)**

crown **(1)**

count **(1)**

Another Vowel Sound

would **(1)**

/ô/ Sound

lawn **(1)**

talk **(1)**

cloth **(1)**

also **(1)**

soft **(1)**

law **(1)**

Name _____

Spelling Spree

Hidden Words Write the Spelling Word that is
hidden in each group of letters. Do not let the
other letters fool you.

Example: e t i t o w n p e *town*

1. p r e s o f t a c   <u>soft **(1 point)**</u>

2. c h a l s o g h e r   <u>also **(1)**</u>

3. l a n r c l o t h   <u>cloth **(1)**</u>

4. r e c l o w n e f   <u>clown **(1)**</u>

Letter Swap Change the underlined letter in each
word to make a Spelling Word. Write the Spelling
Word.

Example: s<u>h</u>all *small*

5. cou<u>r</u>t   <u>count **(1)**</u>

6. <u>d</u>awn   <u>lawn **(1)**</u>

7. c
row<u>s</u>   <u>crown **(1)**</u>

8. <u>s</u>outh   <u>mouth **(1)**</u>

9. tal<u>l</u>   <u>talk **(1)**</u>

10. wor<u>l</u>d   <u>would **(1)**</u>

11. l<u>o</u>w   <u>law **(1)**</u>

12. <u>m</u>ound   <u>sound **(1)**</u>

Assessment Tip: Total **12** Points

Proofreading and Writing

Proofreading Circle the five misspelled Spelling
Words. Then write each word correctly.

WARNING TO MICE!

The monster has had puppies! At last (cownt),

six had been seen. They are now in the city.

Do not think of these dogs as (sawft) and cute.

They tore up a (laun)! They chewed up some

(kloth)! Many mice (woud) fit in one puppy's

mouth. So if you see one, run!

Spelling Words

1. clown
2. lawn
3. talk
4. sound
5. cloth
6. would*
7. also
8. mouth
9. crown
10. soft
11. count
12. law

1. count **(1)**

2. soft **(1)**

3. lawn **(1)**

4. cloth **(1)**

5. would **(1)**

Write a Comparison How big is a mouse? How big
is a dog? What does a mouse eat? What does a dog
eat? How many feet does each animal have? What are
their tails like?

**On a separate piece of paper, write a comparison of
a dog and a mouse. Tell how they are alike and how
they are different. Use Spelling Words from the list.**

Responses will vary. **(5 points)**

Name _____

Find Meaning Using Context

Choose the correct definition for each of the underlined words in the passage. Write the letter of the definition after the number of the word it matches. Use context clues to help you.

a. ran away, fled

b. frightened, alarmed

c. helpful, constructive

d. enjoyment, pleasure

e. shiver or shake

f. relating to a very early time before events were written down

g. carved, as a design on metal or glass

h. very bad, terrible

i. extremely deep place

j. call forth, gather together

    All at once, the volcano began to <u>tremble</u> and rumble. Up
1
from the <u>depths</u> of the earth came the <u>dreadful</u> Dogzilla! This
2   3
monster was millions of years old, from <u>prehistoric</u> times. The
4
mice didn't think they could teach it to do anything <u>positive</u> for
5
their town. Using all the courage they could <u>muster</u>, the mice
6
approached Dogzilla. They hit her with a blast of warm, sudsy
water. The <u>panicking</u> pooch took off at <u>top speed</u>. Delighted,
7
the Big Cheese watched with <u>relish</u> as Dogzilla <u>hightailed</u> it
8   9
out of town. The scary memory of the bubble bath was <u>etched</u>
10
in Dogzilla's mind forever.

1. e **(1)**

2. i **(1)**

3. h **(1)**

4. f **(1)**

5. c **(1)**

6. j **(1)**

7. b **(1)**

8. d **(1)**

9. a **(1)**

10. g **(1)**

Name _____

Writing Possessive Nouns

Rewrite each phrase, using a possessive.

1. the barbecue of the mouse

   the mouse's barbecue **(2 points)**

2. the behavior of the animal

   the animal's behavior **(2)**

3. the barbecue of the mice

   the mice's barbecue **(2)**

4. the shouts of the mayor

   the mayor's shouts **(2)**

5. the smoke of two volcanoes

   the two volcanoes' smoke **(2)**

6. the shouts of the citizens

   the citizens' shouts **(2)**

7. the tail of the cat

   the cat's tail **(2)**

8. the cries of the soldiers

   the soldiers' cries **(2)**

9. the dog belonging to the Smiths

   the Smiths' dog **(2)**

10. the dog belonging to Abigail

    Abigail's dog **(2)**

Name _____

Finding the Possessive

On the line provided, write the noun in parentheses as a possessive noun to complete each sentence. Then write S if the possessive noun is singular, and P if it is plural.

1. The _artist's **(2 points)**_ pictures dazzle the reader. (artist) __S__

2. I think that the _readers' **(2)**_ interest will be high. (readers) __P__

3. An _illustrator's **(2)**_ imagination is clear on every page. (illustrator) __S__

4. The _dog's **(2)**_ expression looks like a smile. (dog) __S__

5. At the end of the story, the _puppies' **(2)**_ faces are adorable. (puppies) __P__

6. Most _monsters' **(2)**_ faces aren't that cute! (monsters) __P__

7. Every _reader's **(2)**_ reaction will be a little different. (reader) __S__

8. All of the _characters' **(2)**_ actions were ridiculous. (characters) __P__

9. I think that our _class's **(2)**_ favorite character is Dogzilla. (class) __S__

10. The book was awarded a prize by the _teachers' **(2)**_ committee. (teachers) __P__

Assessment Tip: Total **20** Points

Name _____

Apostrophes

Rewrite each of the following sentences, adding apostrophes to each incorrectly spelled possessive noun.

1. How would Dav Pilkeys book be different if it were called *Frogzilla*?

   How would Dav Pilkey's book be different if it were called *Frogzilla*?

   (2 points)

2. The city would be crushed by Frogzillas huge feet.

   The city would be crushed by Frogzilla's huge feet. **(2)**

3. The new heros name might be Dennis the Fly.

   The new hero's name might be Dennis the Fly. **(2)**

4. What do you think the flys strategy would be?

   What do you think the fly's strategy would be? **(2)**

5. What are the frogs weaknesses?

   What are the frogs' weaknesses? **(2)**

Name _____

Writing a Journal Entry

**In the space below, write a journal entry for today.
Describe things you see, feel, think about, or remember.
Then use your entry to complete the table below.**

My Daily Journal

Today's Date: _____

Journal entries will vary. **(5 points)**

_____

_____

_____

_____

_____

_____

_____

_____

What I Wrote About Today

Facts	Observations	Feelings	Memories	Ideas
Entries will vary.	Entries will vary.	Entries will vary.	Entries will vary.	Entries will vary.
(2)	(2)	(2)	(2)	(2)

Assessment Tip: Total **15** Points

Name _____

Voice

Suppose one of the puppies wrote this journal entry:

Those silly mice! They think their big barbecue (tommorow) will go off without a hitch. Well, they've had their peace and quiet. Now let's see if they like to play with (puppys!) I'm raring to go, and I'm planning on having lots of fun in Mousopolis tomorrow. And if they (tries) any of that bath stuff on me, we'll just see who can take a licking!

Suppose the Big Cheese wrote this in his journal:

Tomorrow is the first anniversary of the Dogzilla disaster, and that makes me nervous. What (hapened) to Dogzilla? Can we be sure she (don't) come back? Will tomorrow be the day a new monster (destroies) poor Mousopolis yet again? I'm scared!

1. How would you describe the puppy's voice in his entry?

   The puppy is excited and self-confident and is looking forward to

   tomorrow with glee. **(2 points)**

2. How would you describe the Big Cheese's voice in his entry?

   The Big Cheese is worried and frightened and is looking forward to

   tomorrow with dread. **(2)**

In both journal entries, circle examples of grammar and spelling that are not perfect. See circled items in the journal entries. **(2)**

Name _____

Revising Your Story

Reread your story. What do you need to make it better? Use this page to help you decide. Put a checkmark in the box for each sentence that describes your personal narrative.

Rings the Bell!

☐ The beginning catches the reader's interest.

☐ My plot is well developed and will hold the reader's attention.

☐ My characters are interesting. I used many details.

☐ I told enough so the reader can picture the setting.

☐ There are almost no mistakes.

Getting Stronger

☐ The beginning could be more interesting.

☐ My plot isn't always clear. Some parts need more explanation.

☐ The ending doesn't really tell how the problem was solved.

☐ I need to add more details.

☐ There are a few mistakes.

Try Harder

☐ The beginning is boring.

☐ The problem is not clear. I did not tell how it was solved.

☐ I need details that tell about my character and the setting.

Name _____

Using Possessive Nouns

A **possessive noun** shows ownership.
► Add '**s** to make a noun possessive.
► Add just an ' (apostrophe) to make a plural noun that ends with *s* a possessive noun.

Rewrite each phrase, using a possessive noun. Then use the new phrase in a sentence of your own. Sentences will vary.

1. the equipment of the team _the team's equipment_ **(2 points)**

_____

_____

2. the teamwork of the players _the players' teamwork_ **(2)**

_____

_____

3. the orders of the coach _the coach's orders_ **(2)**

_____

_____

4. the roar of the audience _the audience's roar_ **(2)**

_____

_____

5. the songs of the cheerleaders _the cheerleaders' songs_ **(2)**

_____

_____

Name _____

Spelling Words

Look for spelling patterns you have learned to help
you remember the Spelling Words on this page.
Think about the parts that you find hard to spell.

Write the missing letters in the Spelling Words below.

Spelling Words

1. and
2. said
3. goes
4. going
5. some
6. something
7. you
8. your
9. friend
10. school
11. where
12. myself

1. an <u>d</u>____ **(1 point)**

2. s <u>a</u>____ <u>i</u>____ d **(1)**

3. go <u>e</u>____ <u>s</u>____ **(1)**

4. go <u>i</u>____ <u>n</u>____ <u>g</u>____ **(1)**

5. s <u>o</u>____ me **(1)**

6. som <u>e</u>____ thing **(1)**

7. y <u>o</u>____ <u>u</u>____ **(1)**

8. y <u>o</u>____ <u>u</u>____ r ____ **(1)**

9. fr <u>i</u>____ <u>e</u>____ nd **(1)**

10. s <u>c</u>____ <u>h</u>____ ool **(1)**

11. w <u>h</u>____ ere **(1)**

12. m <u>y</u>____ <u>s</u>____ elf **(1)**

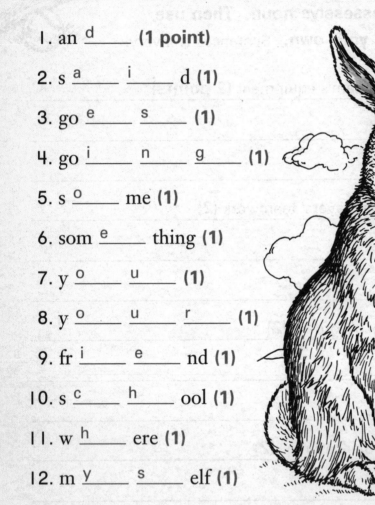

Study List On another sheet of paper, write each
Spelling Word. Check the list to be sure you spell
each word correctly. Order of words may vary. **(2)**

Assessment Tip: Total **14** Points

Name _____

Spelling Spree

The Third Word Write the Spelling Word that belongs in each group.

1. I, me, _myself **(1 point)**_

2. plus, also, _and **(1)**_

3. talked, spoke, _said **(1)**_

4. pal, buddy, _friend **(1)**_

5. their, our, _your **(1)**_

6. moves, runs, _goes **(1)**_

Sentence Fillers Write the Spelling Word that makes the most sense in each sentence below.

7. Do you know _where **(1)**_ soccer practice is tomorrow?

8. I have _some **(1)**_ books about bears that I bought last summer.

9. Our _school **(1)**_ usually lets out at 3 o'clock.

10. When is your class _going **(1)**_ to the library?

11. My brother wrote _something **(1)**_ in my notebook, but I can't read it.

12. Have _you **(1)**_ seen my pet snake anywhere?

Spelling Words

1. and
2. said
3. goes
4. going
5. some
6. something
7. you
8. your
9. friend
10. school
11. where
12. myself

Theme 3: **Incredible Stories** 155

Assessment Tip: Total **12 Points**

Name _____

Proofreading and Writing

Proofreading Circle the four misspelled Spelling Words in the story. Then write each word correctly.

Yesterday, I was on my way into (skool) when I heard something rustling in the bushes. I turned around (an) went over to see what it was. I looked in the spot (were) I had heard the noise, but there was nothing there. Then, from behind me, a voice (sed), "Are you looking for me?" I turned around and found myself face to face with a fox with a sly grin on its face.

1. school **(2 points)**   3. where **(2)**

2. and **(2)**   4. said **(2)**

Incredible Sentences Write four sentences that tell about something incredible. Use a Spelling Word from the list in each one. Sentences will vary. **(4)**

Assessment Tip: Total **12 Points**

Name _____

What Do These Words Mean?

Look up each word in your glossary. Then, in the box above each word, draw a picture that shows the meaning of the word.

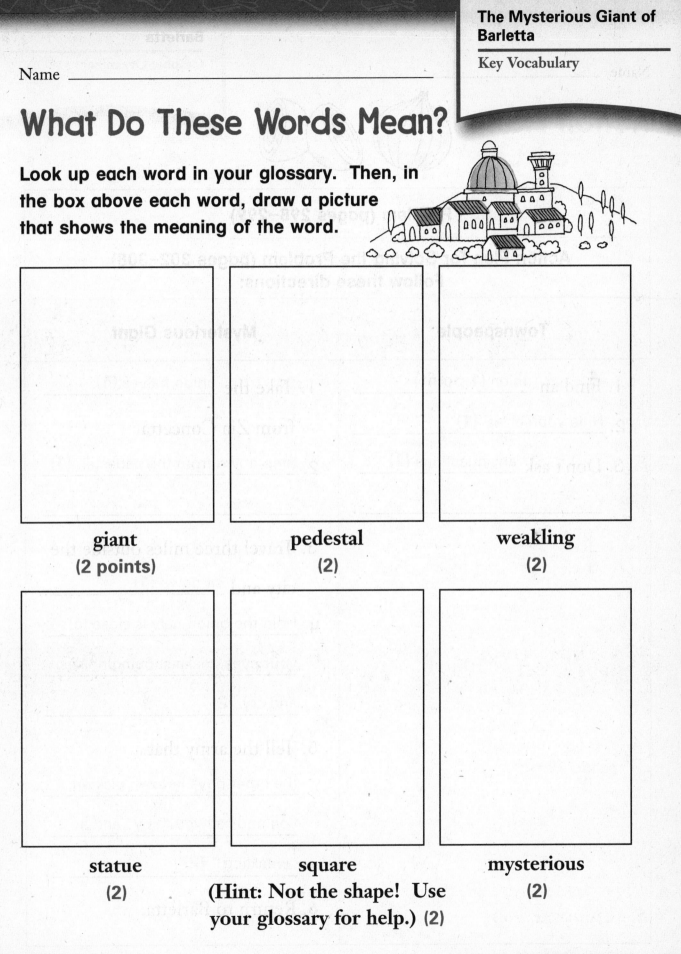

giant **(2 points)**	**pedestal** **(2)**	**weakling** **(2)**
statue **(2)**	**square** **(Hint: Not the shape! Use your glossary for help.) (2)**	**mysterious** **(2)**

Name _____

Action Plan

Problem (pages 298–299)	
Action Plan for Solving the Problem (pages 302–308) **Follow these directions:**	
Townspeople	**Mysterious Giant**

Townspeople

1. Find an ___onion (1 point)___.

2. ___Hide yourselves. (1)___

3. Don't ask ___any questions (1)___

_____.

Mysterious Giant

1. Take the ___onion halves (1)___ from Zia Concetta.

2. ___Step down from the pedestal. (1)___

_____

3. Travel three miles outside the city and ___sit down (1)___.

4. ___Hold the onion halves close to your eyes, make sobbing noises, and cry. (2)___

5. Tell the army that ___the other boys in town pick on you and call you "tiny" and a "weakling." (2)___.

6. Return to Barletta.

Assessment Tip: Total **10** Points

Name _____

Remember the Details

Think about *The Mysterious Giant of Barletta*. Then complete the sentences.

1. The people of Barletta show their love for the Mysterious Giant by

   greeting him, asking him for good luck, playing near him, and, for older boys

   and girls, spending time near him. **(2 points)**

2. The peaceful time for Barletta is over when

   word reaches the town that a large army is on its way. **(2)**

3. Zia Concetta and the Giant figure out a plan to save Barletta. The plan is

   for the Giant to use onion pieces to make himself cry. He must tell the soldiers

   that he's crying because the other boys pick on him since he's so small. **(2)**

4. After the soldiers hear what the Giant says, they wonder

   how big the rest of the townspeople are. **(2)**

5. The army captain decides there is only one thing to do, so they

   turn around and run in the opposite direction of Barletta. **(2)**

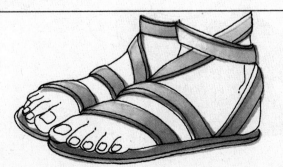

Theme 3: **Incredible Stories**   159
Assessment Tip: Total **10** Points

Name _____

Directions for Fun

Read the directions. Then answer the questions on the next page.

Fingertip Puppets

Act out your favorite folktale or story using puppets you've made yourself. It's easy and fun to do. All you need are an old rubber glove, scissors, glue, marking pens, and some craft supplies.

First, find an old rubber glove that can be cut apart. Each finger will become a puppet. Draw a line about 2 ½ inches below each fingertip of the glove. Cut along the line and then turn the fingertip inside out.

Next, make the puppet look special. Draw a funny face on your puppet. Then glue on hair made from cotton or yarn. Finally, glue on a hat, shirt, or collar made with pieces of felt. You may also want to add beads, buttons, or trims.

Name _____

Directions for Fun continued

Answer each question about making a fingertip puppet.

1. What supplies will you need?

   An old rubber glove, scissors, glue, marking pens, and craft supplies

   like yarn or cotton, felt, beads, buttons, and trims. **(2 points)**

2. After you find an old rubber glove, what do you do?

   Draw a line 2 ½ inches below each fingertip. **(2)**

3. Why should you draw the line before you cut?

   The line shows you where to cut. **(2)**

4. After you cut off the fingertip, what should you do next?

   Turn the fingertip inside out. **(2)**

5. What should you do before you glue on the hair?

   Draw the face. **(2)**

Name _____

Giant Endings

Fill in each blank using the base word and the ending *-er* or *-est*. The base words are in dark type. To solve the puzzle, write the numbered letter from each answer on the line with the matching number.

1. The statue was the t a l l e s t thing
                    5

   in Barletta. **(tall) (1 point)**

2. The statue had been in the square l o n g e r
                                   7

   than anyone could remember. **(long) (1)**

3. To the Giant, late nights were the n i c e s t
                           1

   time of all. **(nice) (1)**

4. The town was q u i e t e r at night
                3

   than at any other time. **(quiet) (1)**

5. The army was s t r o n g e r than
               2   6

   the people of Barletta. **(strong) (1)**

6. The torches were b r i g h t e r
                         4

   than ever. **(bright) (1)**

The Mysterious Giant has a lot of:

c o u r a g e
1 2 3 4 5 6 7

Assessment Tip: Total **6** Points

Vowel + /r/ Sounds

Remember these spelling patterns for the vowel + /r/ sounds:

Patterns		Examples
/är/	**ar**	dark
/îr/	**ear**	clear
/ôr/	**or**	north
/ûr/	**er**	her
	ir	girl
	ur	turn
	or	work

Write each Spelling Word under its vowel + /r/ sounds. Order of answers for each category may vary.

/är/ Sounds

dark **(1 point)**

smart **(1)**

/îr/ Sounds

clear **(1)**

/ôr/ Sounds

north **(1)**

/ûr/ Sounds

girl **(1)**

her **(1)**

work **(1)**

word **(1)**

serve **(1)**

third **(1)**

turn **(1)**

hurt **(1)**

Spelling Spree

Name _____

Questions Write a Spelling Word to answer each question.

1. What direction is opposite to south?
2. How do you feel when you solve a hard problem?
3. What might a car do at a street corner?
4. What do you call a sky without clouds?
5. What is it like outside after sunset?
6. What comes between second and fourth?

1. north **(1 point)**	4. clear **(1)**
2. smart **(1)**	5. dark **(1)**
3. turn **(1)**	6. third **(1)**

Spelling Words

1. girl
2. clear
3. her
4. turn
5. dark
6. work
7. smart
8. word
9. hurt
10. serve
11. north
12. third

Missing Letters Each missing letter fits in ABC order between the other letters. Write the missing letters to spell a Spelling Word.

Example: g __ i n __ p q __ s m __ o *horn*

7. r __ t d __ f q __ s u __ w d __ f   serve **(1 point)** _____

8. g __ i d __ f q __ s   her **(1)** _____

9. v __ x n __ p q __ s j __ l   work **(1)** _____

10. f __ h h __ j q __ s k __ m   girl **(1)** _____

11. v __ x n __ p q __ s c __ e   word **(1)** _____

12. g __ i t __ v q __ s s __ u   hurt **(1)** _____

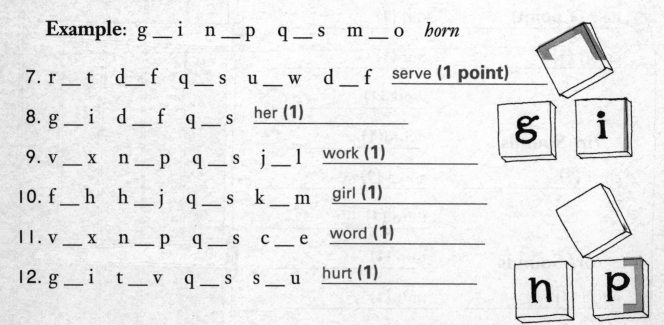

Assessment Tip: Total **12** Points

Name _____

Proofreading and Writing

Proofreading Circle the four misspelled Spelling Words below. Then write each word correctly.

Here is a good way to reach Barletta. Head (noarth) from Naples. At the edge of town, turn right onto the main highway. This road should be pretty (cleer.) Take the (therd) exit after you reach the coast. You should get to Barletta before (darck.)

Spelling Words

1. girl
2. clear
3. her
4. turn
5. dark
6. work
7. smart
8. word
9. hurt
10. serve
11. north
12. third

north **(1 point)** _____ third **(1)** _____

clear **(1)** _____ dark **(1)** _____

Write a Description If you were to make a statue, who would be your subject? Where would it stand so others could see it?

On a separate sheet of paper, write a description of your statue. Tell where it will be placed. Use Spelling Words from the list. Responses will vary. **(4 points)**

Assessment Tip: Total **8 Points**

Name _____

Which Meaning Is Correct?

From the definitions below, choose the correct meaning for the underlined word in each sentence. Write the number of the meaning in the blank provided.

---

bargain *noun* **1.** An agreement between two sides; deal: *We made a bargain to split the chores.* **2.** Something offered or bought at a low price: *The book was a bargain at 25 cents.*

---

hail *verb* **1.** To greet or welcome by calling out: *We hailed our friends as they got off the bus.* **2.** To call or signal to: *I hailed a taxi at the corner* **3.** To congratulate by cheering: *The crowd hailed the hero's return.*

---

settle *verb* **1.** To arrange or decide upon: *Let's settle the argument today.* **2.** To come to rest: *The leaf settled on the grass.* **3.** To make a home or place to live in: *Pioneers settled on the prairie.*

---

1. Every day, the townspeople <u>hailed</u> the Mysterious Giant as they walked to the market. <u>1 **(2 points)**</u>

2. They asked the statue to help them find a good <u>bargain</u> at the market. <u>2 **(2)**</u>

3. Doves flew to the statue and <u>settled</u> on his head. <u>2 **(2)**</u>

4. The Mysterious Giant was <u>hailed</u> as a hero. <u>3 **(2)**</u>

Assessment Tip: Total **8** Points

Name _____

Circling Verbs

Circle the verb in each sentence.

1. The giant statue (stands) in the center of town. **(1 point)**

2. People often (look) at the statue. **(1)**

3. Everyone (loves) the statue. **(1)**

4. Zia Concetta (is) the oldest person in Barletta. **(1)**

5. One day, an enemy army (approaches) the town. **(1)**

6. Everyone (fears) the army of powerful soldiers. **(1)**

7. The soldiers (march) toward the town. **(1)**

8. The mysterious statue (hops) off his pedestal. **(1)**

9. He (asks) for three special things. **(1)**

10. The giant statue (cries) because of the onion's smell. **(1)**

Assessment Tip: Total **10 Points**

Name _____

Finding Verbs

Find the verb in each sentence, and write it on the line at the right.

1. In this story, the giant statue leaps off its pedestal. <u>leaps **(1 point)**</u>

2. The people believe in the giant. <u>believe **(1)**</u>

3. Clearly, the giant cares about the town of Barletta. <u>cares **(1)**</u>

4. Unfortunately, an army attacks the town. <u>attacks **(1)**</u>

5. The people quickly identify the trouble. <u>identify **(1)**</u>

6. With a little thought, the giant solves the problem. <u>solves **(1)**</u>

7. He cuts an onion into two pieces. <u>cuts **(1)**</u>

8. The tears run down his face. <u>run **(1)**</u>

9. The army fears the giant and his friends. <u>fears **(1)**</u>

10. At the end of the story, the soldiers leave town. <u>leave **(1)**</u>

Use this chart to classify the verbs from the sentences above.

Physical Action	Mental Action
leaps **(1)**	believe **(1)**
attacks **(1)**	cares **(1)**
cuts **(1)**	identify **(1)**
run **(1)**	solves **(1)**
leave **(1)**	fears **(1)**

Assessment Tip: Total **20** Points

Name _____

Using Exact Verbs

Circle the verb in each sentence. Then think of an exact verb to make the sentence more interesting. Rewrite the sentence using your exact verb. Student's verb choices will vary. Possible responses given.

1. An army of powerful soldiers appears.

   An army of powerful soldiers **attacks**. **(2 points)**

2. One night, Zia Concetta goes to the statue.

   One night, Zia Concetta **rushes** to the statue. **(2)**

3. The giant statue moves off the pedestal.

   The giant statue **leaps** off the pedestal. **(2)**

4. The statue's clever plan beats the large army.

   The statue's clever plan **outsmarts** the large army. **(2)**

5. Today, the statue still is in Barletta, Italy.

   Today, the statue still **stands** in Barletta, Italy. **(2)**

Name _____

Write a Thank-You Note

Use this outline to write a thank-you letter for a gift you have been given. When you have finished your letter, answer the questions below. Responses will vary.

Address/Date **(2 points)** _____

Greeting **(2)** _____

Body   Students should name the gift in the first sentence. **(2)**
Students should tell why they enjoyed receiving and using the gift.

(2) _____

Closing **(2)** _____

Signature **(2)** _____

What did you say in your letter to explain why the gift is important to you?

Responses will vary. **(2)**

_____

What did you say in your letter to make the giver feel good about giving the gift?

Responses will vary. **(2)**

_____

Assessment Tip: Total **16** Points

Name _____

Using Commas for Direct Address

What if in all the excitement at Barletta, no one remembered to thank the vegetable store owner for supplying the very important onion?

Suppose that the thank-you note has now been written, but it needs proofreading. Read the note. Add commas where they belong, before or after the name of the person being addressed.

(Each comma in the letter is worth **2 points**.)

Dear Sir,

    We the people of Barletta thank you for supplying the onion that made our giant cry! Sir, without your onion, our whole plan might have failed miserably. We were ready to run from Barletta, but you, Sir, stayed bravely in your shop, guarding your vegetables. When your city needed you, you were ready, Sir. When we said, "Sir, find us an onion," you knew just what to do. Now everyone will always say that it was because of you and your onion that Barletta was saved. Sir, you have reason to be proud!

                                              Sincerely,
                                              The Mayor

Name _____

Farm Words

Vocabulary

appetite
chores
harvested
hitched
plow
sown
tended

Write each word next to its definition.

1. gathered or picked harvested (**1 point**)

2. planted sown (**1**)

3. hunger appetite (**1**)

4. jobs chores (**1**)

5. break up and turn over dirt plow (**1**)

6. took care of tended (**1**)

7. tied or fastened hitched (**1**)

Write sentences to answer these questions. Answers will vary.

8. When you have a big appetite, what do you do?

_____ (**1**) _____

9. What kinds of fruits or vegetables have you harvested?

_____ (**1**) _____

10. What are your favorite chores? What chores don't you like to do?

_____ (**1**) _____

Assessment Tip: Total 10 Points

Name _____

Conclusions Chart

Sample responses are provided.

Story Details		Story Details		Conclusion
(page 320) Pa raises corn, peas, barley, wheat, and many farm animals.	+	(Page 320) He says he has no time for make believe. **(1 point)**	=	Pa works hard on the farm. **(1)**
(page 323; it's not a rock.) It's too round, smooth and not hard enough. **(1 point)**	+	(page 325) A tiny dragon hatches from it. **(1)**	=	(What's in Miller's Cave) a dragon egg **(1)**
(page 328; Hank's size) Hank grows to be as big as a barn from tail to snout. **(1)**	+	(Page 328) Hank has wings. **(1)**	=	(What Hank looks like) extraordinary; unusual **(2)**
(page 334) He starts drawing crowds and attention. **(2)**	+	(page 337) Hank feels right at home on the island. **(2)**	=	(Hank's fate) He's better off living on the dragon-shaped island. **(2)**

Assessment Tip: Total **15** Points

Name _____

The Dragon's Tale

Tell what happened in *Raising Dragons*.
Complete each sentence to finish the story.
Sample answers are provided.

One day a little girl found what looked like a big rock. It was

an egg. She kept wondering <u>what was coming out of the egg. **(1 point)**</u>

_____.

One night she heard <u>a loud noise **(1)**</u>.

Then the little girl saw <u>a tiny dragon **(1)**</u>.

Of course, the girl loved Hank. Each day she fed him and

<u>took care of him **(1)**</u>_____.

Soon he was part of their lives.

Hank helped around the farm. He saved Ma's tomatoes. He

also saved the corn by <u>setting fire to the field and making popcorn. **(1)**</u>

_____.

Then Hank got too much attention. So the girl took Hank to

<u>a dragon-shaped island **(1)**</u>_____. She knew

Hank could live there because <u>he got along well with the other</u>

<u>dragons **(1)**</u>_____.

But Hank surprised the little girl with <u>more dragon eggs to take</u>

<u>home **(1)**</u>_____.

174   Theme 3: **Incredible Stories**
Assessment Tip: Total **8 Points**

Name _____

Conclusions from Clues

Read these details about dragons. Then fill in the chart on the next page.

What Dragons Are Really Like

► Dragons have skin much like snakes, lizards, and other reptiles. Since they are cold-blooded, dragons like to live in warm spots.

► Each spring, dragons lay eggs in nests they build. Their nests are made from the same materials that birds use.

► Dragons can fly, but their wings are not at all like birds' wings. They are more like large, leathery bat wings.

► Usually, dragons will not harm people. They only eat frogs, bugs, and fish. Some dragons have been trained to be useful. They pull plows and do other tasks that horses do.

► Dragons do not breathe fire. However, their teeth are larger than a shark's, and they will use them to keep their babies safe.

Name _____

Conclusions from Clues continued

Read each conclusion. Decide if it is correct, and write
YES or *NO*. Write the clues that helped
you decide.

Conclusions	Correct Conclusion? (Yes or No)	Story Clues
Dragon skin is scaly.	Yes **(1 point)**	Their skin is much like that of a snake's or lizard's. **(2)**
Dragon nests are made of twigs, sticks, and grasses.	Yes **(1)**	Their nests are made from the same materials that birds use. **(2)**
Dragon wings have feathers.	No **(1)**	Their wings are not like birds' wings. They are more like large, leathery bat wings. **(2)**
Dragons can be trained to carry riders.	Yes **(1)**	They can be trained to do things that horses can do. **(2)**
Dragons never bite.	No **(1)**	They will use their teeth to keep their babies safe. **(2)**

Assessment Tip: Total **15** Points

Name _____

Happy Endings

Choose a word from the box to match each picture clue.
Write the word on the line.

Word Bank

proudly	brightly	leaky	cloudy	beastly
furry	lovely	bumpy	rainy	hairy

1. + y = <u>r</u> <u>a</u> <u>i</u> <u>n</u> <u>y</u> **(1 point)**

2. + ly = <u>b</u> <u>r</u> <u>i</u> <u>g</u> <u>h</u> <u>t</u> <u>l</u> <u>y</u> **(1)**

3. + y = <u>c</u> <u>l</u> <u>o</u> <u>u</u> <u>d</u> <u>y</u> **(1)**

4. + ly = <u>b</u> <u>e</u> <u>a</u> <u>s</u> <u>t</u> <u>l</u> <u>y</u> **(1)**

5. + y = <u>b</u> <u>u</u> <u>m</u> <u>p</u> <u>y</u> **(1)**

6. + ly = <u>l</u> <u>o</u> <u>v</u> <u>e</u> <u>l</u> <u>y</u> **(1)**

Name _____

The /j/, /k/, and /kw/ Sounds

▶ The /j/ sound can be spelled with the consonant *j* or with the consonant *g* followed by *e* or *y*.

   /j/ **j**eans, lar**ge**, **g**y**m**

▶ The starred word *judge* has two /j/ sounds in it. The first /j/ sound is spelled *j*, and the second is spelled *dge*.

▶ The /k/ sound can be spelled with *k*, *ck*, or *c*. The /kw/ sounds can be spelled with the *qu* pattern.

   /k/ par**k**, qui**ck**, pi**c**ni**c**   /kw/ s**qu**eeze

Spelling Words
1. large
2. gym
3. skin
4. quick
5. picnic
6. judge
7. park
8. jeans
9. crack
10. orange
11. second
12. squeeze

Write the Spelling Words that have the /j/ sound in them. Then write the Spelling Words that have the /k/ or /kw/ sounds in them.

/j/ Sound	/k/ or /kw/ Sounds
large **(1 point)**	skin **(1)**
gym **(1)**	quick **(1)**
judge **(1)**	picnic **(1)**
jeans **(1)**	park **(1)**
orange **(1)**	crack **(1)**
	second **(1)**
	squeeze **(1)**

Assessment Tip: Total **12** Points

Name _____

Spelling Spree

Silly Rhymes **Write a Spelling Word to complete each sentence. The answer rhymes with the underlined word.**

Spelling Words

1. large
2. gym
3. skin
4. quick
5. picnic
6. judge
7. park
8. jeans
9. crack
10. orange
11. second
12. squeeze

1. The hungry _____ ate some <u>fudge</u>.

2. Birds in the _____ sleep after <u>dark</u>.

3. I dropped baked <u>beans</u> on my new _____ .

4. There is a _____ in the train <u>track</u>.

5. Can more <u>bees</u> _____ into the hive?

6. A _____ <u>barge</u> is on the river.

1. judge **(1 point)**   4. crack **(1)**

2. park **(1)**   5. squeeze **(1)**

3. jeans **(1)**   6. large **(1)**

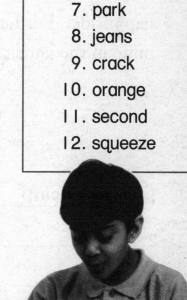

Letter Math **Solve each problem by using a Spelling Word.**

> **Example:** joke – ke + b = *job*

7. pick – k + nic = picnic **(1)**

8. or + angel – l = orange **(1)**

9. s + king – g = skin **(1)**   11. sec + fond – f = second **(1)**

10. quit – t + ck = quick **(1)**   12. edgy – ed + m = gym **(1)**

Name _____

Proofreading and Writing

Proofreading Circle the five misspelled Spelling Words. Then write each word correctly.

> Dear Diary,
>   Today we went to the zoo. We saw (larje) snakes and turtles. One turtle splashed water on my (geans!) There was a dragon cage, but it was empty. I guess the dragons were taking a (quik) nap inside. For lunch we had a (picnick) I ate mine in the (parc.)

Spelling Words
1. large
2. gym
3. skin
4. quick
5. picnic
6. judge
7. park
8. jeans
9. crack
10. orange
11. second
12. squeeze

1. large **(1 point)**
2. jeans **(1)**
3. quick **(1)**
4. picnic **(1)**
5. park **(1)**

Write a List of Rules A baby dragon would need a lot of care. What rules should someone follow when raising a dragon?

On a separate sheet of paper, write a list of rules for taking care of a dragon. Use Spelling Words from the list.

Responses will vary. **(5)**

Assessment Tip: Total **10** Points

Name _____

Say It Right!

Pronunciation Key			
ă map	ĭ pit	oi **oil**	th **bath**
ā pay	ī ride	ŏŏ **book**	_th_ **bathe**
â care	î **fierce**	ōō **boot**	ə **ago, item,**
ä father	ŏ pot	ou **out**	**pencil, atom,**
ĕ pet	ō **go**	ŭ cup	**circus**
ē be	ô paw, for	û fur	

Look at the vowel sound in the words below. Then look at the Pronunciation Key and find the sample word with the same vowel sound. Write the word on the line.

1. **must** (mŭst) <u>cup **(1 point)**</u>

2. **dirt** (dûrt) <u>fur **(1)**</u>

3. **breath** (brĕth) <u>pet **(1)**</u>

4. **path** (păth) <u>map **(1)**</u>

5. **chew** (chōō) <u>boot **(1)**</u>

6. **self** (sĕlf) <u>pet **(1)**</u>

7. **dear** (dîr) <u>fierce **(1)**</u>

8. **pair** (pâr) <u>care **(1)**</u>

9. **meal** (mîl) <u>fierce **(1)**</u>

10. **stay** (stā) <u>pay **(1)**</u>

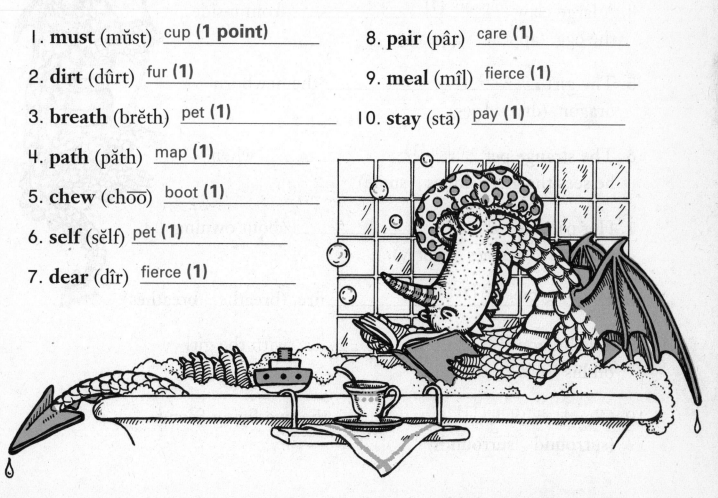

Name _____

Looking for the Present

**Read each sentence. Choose the correct verb
form and write it on the line to complete the sentence.**

1. This story ___tells **(1 point)**___ about a girl
   and her pet dragon. (tell   tells)

2. The dog ___barks **(1)**___ when it sees
   the giant egg. (barks   bark)

3. The neighbors ___watch **(1)**___ the egg
   hatching. (watch   watches)

4. A large claw ___appears **(1)**___ from inside
   the egg. (appear   appears)

5. The girl ___dries **(1)**___ the newborn
   dragon. (dry   dries)

6. The strange pet ___smiles **(1)**___ when
   he sees the girl. (smiles   smile)

7. Her parents ___worry **(1)**___ about owning
   a dragon. (worries   worry)

8. Dragons ___breathe **(1)**___ fire. (breathe   breathes)

9. The dragon ___flies **(1)**___ with the girl
   on his back. (flies fly)

10. Clouds ___surround **(1)**___ the two flying friends.
    (surround   surrounds)

Assessment Tip: Total **10** Points

Name _____

Choosing the Present

Read each sentence. Then write the correct present-time form of the verb in parentheses.

1. A smart girl __raises **(1)**_____ a pet dragon. (raise)

2. The chickens __cluck **(1)**_____ when they see the baby dragon. (cluck)

3. All animals __need **(1)**_____ to eat. (need)

4. This dragon __munches **(1)**_____ on fish, frogs, eels, and insects. (munch)

5. The strange creature __tries **(1)**_____ to be a good friend. (try)

6. The friends __cross **(1)**_____ the farm together. (cross)

7. The dragon __helps **(1)**_____ with daily chores. (help)

8. His hot breath __pops **(1)**_____ the corn in the field. (pop)

9. Customers __buy **(1)**_____ the dragon's popcorn. (buy)

10. The girl __cries **(1)**_____ when the dragon leaves. (cry)

Name _____

Subject-Verb Agreement

**Proofread these paragraphs. Correct
errors in subject-verb agreement.
Circle verbs that are not in the correct time.
Then rewrite the paragraphs on the lines provided.** Each word
is **1 point**.

Benjamin wakes at sunrise. He (look) outside his apartment
window. At first, he (see) only the sun. Then he (spot) five black dots
in the distance. The dots (grows) bigger and bigger. Suddenly, Ben's
jaw (drop) wide open. Five big black dragons (flies) outside his window.

The dragons (calls) to Benjamin. "Come fly with us!" they shout.
Benjamin (think) about it. In a few seconds, he (decide). In a flash, he
(jump) onto one of the dragons. The new friends (zooms) into the air.
Benjamin laughs and (wonder) what will happen next.

Benjamin wakes at sunrise. He **looks** outside his apartment window. At

first, he **sees** only the sun. Then he **spots** five black dots in the distance.

The dots **grow** bigger and bigger. Suddenly, Ben's jaw **drops** wide open.

Five big black dragons **fly** outside his window.

The dragons **call** to Benjamin. "Come fly with us!" they shout.

Benjamin **thinks** about it. In a few seconds, he **decides**. In a flash, he

jumps onto one of the dragons. The new friends **zoom** into the air.

Benjamin laughs and **wonders** what will happen next.

Assessment Tip: Total **12** Points

Name _____

Planning Your Writing

Use this page to plan your opinion. Then number your reasons or facts in the order you will use them.

Answers will vary.

Topic: (2 points) _____

_____

_____

Topic Sentence: (2) _____

_____

_____

Reason/Fact: (2)

_____

_____

_____

Reason/Fact: (2)

_____

_____

_____

Reason/Fact: (2)

_____

_____

_____

Reason/Fact: (2)

_____

_____

_____

Name _____

Using Commas with Introductory Phrases

Select the introductory group of words from the box that best completes each sentence.

for example	first of all	in addition
in conclusion	most important	

Cats Are the Best Pets

I think cats are the best pets. (1)
_First of all, **(1 point)**_____ they are fun to watch.

(2) _For example, **(1)**_____ if you roll a ball in

front of it, a cat will bat it around the house.

(3) _In addition, **(1)**_____ cats like to play with

string for hours. (4) _Most important, **(1)**_____ cats

are good companions. They follow you around the house,

and they sleep in your lap. (5) _In conclusion, **(1)**_____

those are the reasons why I think cats are the best pets!

Name _____

A Garden of Words

Circle the word that best completes each sentence. Then write the word in the blank.

1. The elephants were so large they were _awesome_ **(1) point)** .
   A. impossible   C. (awesome) **(1)**
   B. weak   D. smart

2. My teacher _convinced_ **(1)** me that some kinds of plants can eat insects.
   A. discovered   C. rewarded
   B. disappeared   D. (convinced) **(1)**

3. I saw a bird in a tree, but it flew off and _disappeared_ **(1)** .
   A. (disappeared) **(1)** C. grew
   B. discovered   D. walked

4. In the pond, I _discovered_ **(1)** a frog that looked like a leaf.
   A. thought   C. convinced
   B. (discovered) **(1)**   D. read

5. We thought the lion's loud roar was _incredible_ **(1)** .
   A. quiet   C. (incredible) **(1)**
   B. tiny   D. impossible

6. It was almost _impossible_ **(1)** to see

   the white polar bear sitting in the white snow.
   A. best   C. incredible
   B. awesome   D. (impossible) **(1)**

Name _____

Story Map

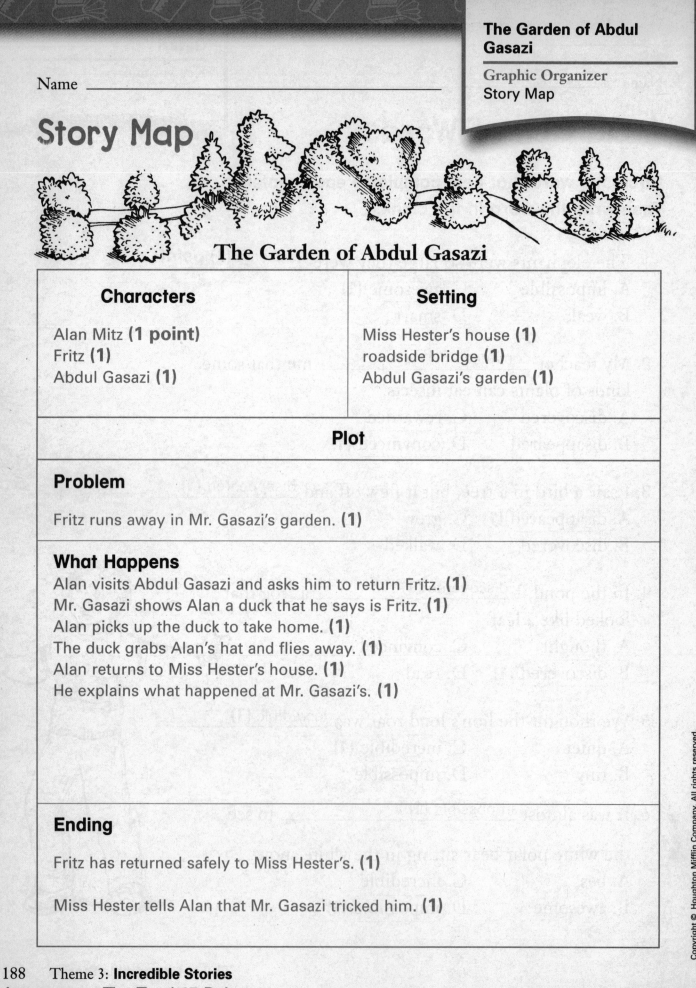

The Garden of Abdul Gasazi

Characters	Setting
Alan Mitz **(1 point)**	Miss Hester's house **(1)**
Fritz **(1)**	roadside bridge **(1)**
Abdul Gasazi **(1)**	Abdul Gasazi's garden **(1)**

Plot

Problem

Fritz runs away in Mr. Gasazi's garden. **(1)**

What Happens

Alan visits Abdul Gasazi and asks him to return Fritz. **(1)**
Mr. Gasazi shows Alan a duck that he says is Fritz. **(1)**
Alan picks up the duck to take home. **(1)**
The duck grabs Alan's hat and flies away. **(1)**
Alan returns to Miss Hester's house. **(1)**
He explains what happened at Mr. Gasazi's. **(1)**

Ending

Fritz has returned safely to Miss Hester's. **(1)**

Miss Hester tells Alan that Mr. Gasazi tricked him. **(1)**

Name _____

Mr. Gasazi's Garden!

Complete each sentence with an event from
The Garden of Abdul Gasazi. **Then explain how**
you feel about the way the story ends.

Sample answers are provided.

1. Miss Hester must visit Cousin Eunice, so she asks

   Alan Mitz to watch Fritz. **(1 point)** _____

2. When Alan takes Fritz for a walk,

   Fritz runs away in the Abdul Gasazi's garden. **(1)** _____

3. As Alan searches for Fritz, he finds Mr. Gasazi's home. **(1)**

4. The magician tells Alan that he has turned Fritz into a duck. **(1)**

   _____

5. As Alan leaves, the duck flies off with his hat. **(1)** _____

6. When Alan returns to Miss Hester's, Fritz is already there at

   the house. **(1)** _____

7. Miss Hester tells Alan that Mr. Gasazi played a trick on him. **(1)**

8. After Alan leaves, Miss Hester tells Fritz that he is a bad dog

   because he has Alan's hat. **(1)** _____

My Feelings About the Ending:

Answers will vary. **(2)** _____

_____

Name _____

The Shape of a Story

Read the story below.

Rescuing Dolly

One cold morning as Keisha walked her dog, Vista, she noticed fresh tracks in the snow. A minute later, a small, spotted dog appeared by the river. With no tag or collar, it clearly was lost. It stared hopefully at Keisha and shivered in the cold. Then Vista barked, and the dog ran off. "It's much too cold for a dog to stay outside for long," Keisha thought. "I've got to do something, but Vista will keep scaring it away."

So Keisha headed for home. She told her mother about the lost dog, and together they returned to the river to find it.

Keisha was almost ready to give up, but at last she spotted the dog. Keisha called to it, but it jumped onto a rock. Then Keisha knelt down. The little dog leaped into her arms and began licking her face.

Weeks later, the little dog's owner still could not be found. So that is how Dolly, the little dog, came to be part of Keisha's family.

Name _____

The Shape of a Story continued

Fill in this story map with details from "Rescuing Dolly."

Characters	Setting
1. Keisha **(1 point)**	the snowy riverbank **(1)**
2. the lost dog **(1)**	

Plot

Problem

Keisha wants to save the lost dog. **(1)**

What Happens

1. She must take Vista home. **(1)**

2. She and her mother return to the river to look for it. **(1)**

3. She calls it, but the dog jumps onto a rock. **(1)**

4. Keisha kneels down. **(1)**

Ending

1. The dog jumps into Keisha's arms. **(1)**

2. Dolly, the dog, becomes part of Keisha's family. **(1)**

Name _____

Playing with Prefixes

On each line, write a word that begins with the prefix *un-*, *dis-*, or *non-* and matches the definition. Then find and circle all eight words in the word search.

1. not locked __unlocked__ **(1 point)**

2. not fiction __nonfiction__ **(1)**

3. the opposite of agree __disagree__ **(1)**

4. not able __unable__ **(1)**

5. the opposite of appear __disappear__ **(1)**

6. not usual __unusual__ **(1)**

7. not fair __unfair__ **(1)**

8. not making sense __nonsense__ **(1)**

```
K N O N F I C T I O N D A D F P E P
D E R W H Y N E Z G Q J X H G H T V
I Z W U C Q X U S Y C Y S S V M Z C
S T V A N L N O N S E N S E Z P G Z
A N P K A L M B S U I G I V K A O R
P V N O W J O O D G S P H Q M H M Z
P T G J G Z O C R S S U N F A I R
E R Y X W L P F K X M P A Z H Z A R
A H E R J Q M W M E G V T L M O J E
R E U N A B L E L P D I S A G R E E
```

(1 point per word in word search)

Assessment Tip: Total **16** Points

Name _____

Homophones

Homophones are words that sound the same but have different spellings and meanings. When you spell a homophone, think about the meaning of the word you want to write.

Homophone	Meaning
/noō/ **new**	not old
/noō/ **kn**ew	understood

Write the four pairs of Spelling Words that are homophones. Order of answers may vary.

hear **(1 point)**   its **(1)**

here **(1)**   it's **(1)**

new **(1)**   our **(1)**

knew **(1)**   hour **(1)**

Now write the three Spelling Words that are homophones. Order of answers may vary.

there **(1 point)**

their **(1)**

they're **(1)**

Spelling Words

1. hear
2. here
3. new
4. knew
5. its
6. it's
7. our
8. hour
9. there
10. their
11. they're

Assessment Tip: Total **11** Points

Name _____

Spelling Spree

Quotation Caper Write the Spelling Word that best completes each quotation that might have come from the story.

1. "We magicians never reveal _____ secrets," said Mr. Gasazi.

2. "Your hat is not in _____ usual place," said Miss Hester.

3. "The ducks have flown back to _____ pond," said Alan.

4. "Fritz, come back _____ !" called Alan.

5. "Dogs should know that _____ not welcome here," grumbled Gasazi.

1. our **(1 point)**   4. here **(1)**

2. its **(1)**   5. they're **(1)**

3. their **(1)**

In Another Word Write a Spelling Word to replace each expression.

6. get wind of   hear **(1)**

7. hot off the press   new **(1)**

8. over yonder   there **(1)**

9. got the picture   knew **(1)**

Assessment Tip: Total **9** Points

Name _____

Proofreading and Writing

Proofreading Suppose that Alan keeps a journal. Circle the five misspelled Spelling Words in this entry. Then write each word correctly.

Spelling Words

1. hear
2. here
3. new
4. knew
5. its
6. it's
7. our
8. hour
9. there
10. their
11. they're

June 3: Today I had a strange adventure. It was in a magician's garden. Miss Hester's dog Fritz ran in (their.) I (knue) we were in trouble when I read the sign: "No dogs allowed." I chased Fritz for at least an (our.) I think (its') possible that the magician turned Fritz into a duck! When I came back (heere,) no one believed my story.

1. there **(1 point)** _____
2. knew **(1)** _____
3. hour **(1)** _____
4. it's **(1)** _____
5. here **(1)** _____

Write a Plan Abdul Gasazi had some amazing trees in his garden. If you could plan a garden, what would you plant in it? Where would you plant things?

On a separate sheet of paper, draw a picture of your garden. Then write a plan for it. Tell what you would plant, and where. Use Spelling Words from the list. Responses will vary. **(5 points)**

Name _____

Ask Your Friendly Thesaurus!

For each underlined word in the following sentences, choose a better word or words from the thesaurus entry. Write your answers in the blanks provided. Some words may have more than one answer.

Thesaurus Entries

1. **funny:** silly, unusual, curious, laughable
2. **pulled:** strained, dragged, stretched, heaved
3. **ran:** darted, flowed, fled, hurried
4. **tired:** exhausted, faint, worn, wilting
5. **walking:** strolling, trotting, striding, stomping
6. **shouted:** called, bellowed, howled, bawled

1. Fritz stopped chewing the furniture and fell asleep,

   completely <u>tired</u>. word from item 4 **(1 point)** _____

2. Alan fastened Fritz's leash and the dog <u>pulled</u> him out of

   the house. word from item 2 **(1)** _____

3. Fritz <u>ran</u> straight through the open door.

   word from item 3 **(1)** _____

4. Gasazi <u>shouted</u> that he had turned the dogs into ducks!

   word from item 6 **(1)** _____

5. Alan felt <u>funny</u> when he thought the magician had fooled

   him. word from item 1 **(1)** _____

6. Fritz came <u>walking</u> up the front steps with Alan's hat.

   word from item 5 **(1)** _____

Assessment Tip: Total **6** Points

Name _____

Choosing Time

**Choose the correct verb form in parentheses and
write it on the line provided to complete the sentence.**

1. Tomorrow Alan <u>will take **(1)**</u> Fritz for
a walk. (takes   will take)

2. Yesterday Alan <u>searched **(1)**</u> for Fritz.
(searched   will search)

3. Yesterday in the garden, Fritz <u>bumped **(1)**</u>
into Abdul. (bumped   will bump)

4. Tomorrow Alan <u>will climb **(1)**</u> the stairs.
(climbed   will climb)

5. Yesterday the ducks <u>flapped **(1)**</u>
their wings. (flapped   will flap)

**Complete the chart by supplying past and
future time for each of the verbs given.**

Verb	Past Time	Future Time
try	tried **(1)**	will try **(1)**
race	raced **(1)**	will race **(1)**
disappear	disappeared **(1)**	will disappear **(1)**
drag	dragged **(1)**	will drag **(1)**
bolt	bolted **(1)**	will bolt **(1)**

Assessment Tip: Total **15** Points

Name _____

Writing Past and Future

Read each sentence. Then write the sentence in past time and future time.

1. Alan walks Fritz.

   Past: Alan walked Fritz. **(1 point)**

   Future: Alan will walk Fritz. **(1)**

2. He hurries after the dog.

   Past: He hurried after the dog. **(1)**

   Future: He will hurry after the dog. **(1)**

3. Alan discovers the magician.

   Past: Alan discovered the magician. **(1)**

   Future: Alan will discover the magician. **(1)**

4. Abdul shows Alan a duck.

   Past: Abdul showed Alan a duck. **(1)**

   Future: Abdul will show Alan a duck. **(1)**

5. The duck grabs Alan's hat.

   Past: The duck grabbed Alan's hat. **(1)**

   Future: The duck will grab Alan's hat. **(1)**

Assessment Tip: Total **10** Points

Name _____

Keeping Verbs Consistent

Read this story. The paragraphs mix up the past, the present, and the future. The story takes place in the past. Circle any verbs that are not in past time. Then write the verbs correctly on the lines below. Each verb is **1 point**.

I visited a strange garden yesterday. The bushes (look) like different animals. A giant green elephant (watches) the main path. I discovered a hidden path. I (will follow) the trail.

A strange noise (sounds) behind me. I turned around. The elephant (moves!) Then the giant plant (faces) in the other direction.

I (decide) to leave the weird garden. I (try) to find my way out. I looked everywhere. The paths twisted and turned.

I (turn) around again. The elephant (watches) me. I (step) farther into the garden. The elephant stared.

Finally, I (uncover) a hidden gate. I (hurry) toward it. The elephant (appears) in front of me. I raced out of the garden. Then I (glance) back. The garden (is) gone.

looked	moved	turned	hurried
watched	faced	watched	appeared
followed	decided	stepped	glanced
sounded	tried	uncovered	was

Theme 3: **Incredible Stories**   199
Assessment Tip: Total **16** Points

Writing Dialogue

Write a dialogue, or a conversation between two or more characters in a story. Try to make the dialogue sound as if real people are talking. Use quotation marks, capital letters, and commas in your dialogue. Choose one of the following groups of characters for your dialogue:

▶ Alan and Miss Hester
▶ Alan and Abdul Gasazi
▶ Miss Hester and Abdul Gasazi
▶ Alan, Miss Hester, and Abdul Gasazi
▶ Two characters from another story of your choice

Dialogues will vary. **(10 points)**

_____

_____

_____

_____

_____

_____

_____

_____

_____

_____

_____

Name _____

Write Quotations Right!

Rewrite each of the following sentences of dialogue that might have taken place. Add quotation marks, capital letters, or commas.

1. Miss Hester said please stay with Fritz and give him his afternoon walk.

   Miss Hester said, "Please stay with Fritz and give him his afternoon

   walk." **(2 points)**

2. don't chew on the furniture, Fritz Alan said angrily.

   "Don't chew on the furniture, Fritz," Alan said angrily. **(2)**

3. please, Fritz Alan exclaimed don't go running off into that garden!

   "Please, Fritz," Alan exclaimed, "don't go running off into that garden!" **(2)**

4. Alan said if you have Fritz, Mr. Gasazi, would you please give him back?

   Alan said, "If you have Fritz, Mr. Gasazi, would you please give him back?" **(2)**

5. something terrible has happened, Miss Hester Alan blurted out. your dog ran away, and Mr. Gasazi turned him into a duck!

   "Something terrible has happened, Miss Hester," Alan blurted out. "Your dog

   ran away, and Mr. Gasazi turned him into a duck!" **(2)**

Theme 3: **Incredible Stories**   201

Assessment Tip: Total **10** Points

Name _____

Writing a Personal Response

Use the test-taking strategies and tips you have learned to help you answer this kind of question. Take the time you need to decide which topic you will write about and to write an answer. Then read your response and see how you may make it better. This practice will help you when you take this kind of test.

Write one or two paragraphs about one of the following topics.

a. You have read *The Mysterious Giant of Barletta*. If you could choose a statue or something else to come to life, what would it be? Tell why you would choose it and how it might act.

b. Zia Concetta said *"grazie"* (thank you) to the Mysterious Giant. In what other ways do you think the townspeople could thank the Giant? How do you thank people for nice things they have done for you?

Answers will vary. **(15 Points)**

_____

_____

_____

_____

_____

_____

_____

_____

Name _____

Writing a Personal Response

continued

Read your answer. Check to be sure that it

- sticks to the topic.
- is well organized.
- has details that support your answer.
- has vivid and exact words.
- has few mistakes in capitalization, punctuation, grammar, or spelling.

Now pick one way you can improve your response.
Make your changes below.

Answers will vary. **(5)**

_____

_____

_____

_____

_____

_____

_____

_____

_____

_____

Assessment Tip: Total **20** Points

Name _____

Name _____

Spelling Review

Write each Spelling Word. Then circle six words that are homophone pairs. Order of answers may vary.

1. word **(1 point)**
2. sound **(1)**
3. clear **(1)**
4. also **(1)**
5. soft **(1)**
6. crack **(1)**
7. lawn **(1)**
8. crown **(1)**
9. girl **(1)**
10. (knew) **(1) / (1)**
11. (here) **(1) / (1)**
12. turn **(1)**
13. dark **(1)**
14. north **(1)**
15. orange **(1)**
16. her **(1)**
17. skin **(1)**
18. (hear) **(1) / (1)**
19. squeeze **(1)**
20. gym **(1)**
21. second **(1)**
22. jeans **(1)**
23. (hour) **(1) / (1)**
24. (our) **(1) / (1)**
25. (new) **(1) / (1)**

Spelling Words

1. word
2. sound
3. clear
4. also
5. soft
6. crack
7. lawn
8. crown
9. girl
10. knew
11. here
12. turn
13. dark
14. north
15. orange
16. her
17. skin
18. hear
19. squeeze
20. gym
21. second
22. jeans
23. hour
24. our
25. new

Name _____

Spelling Spree

Puzzle Play Write a Spelling Word for each clue.
Then use the letters in the boxes to spell a word
about what a dragon is like.

Spelling Words

1. sound
2. lawn
3. crown
4. girl
5. skin
6. crack
7. gym
8. orange
9. second
10. jeans
11. hear
12. hour

1. this covers your body s k i n **(1)**

2. first, —, third s e c o n d **(1)**

3. heavy blue pants j e a n s **(1)**

4. 60 minutes h o u r **(1)**

5. a large indoor play area g y m **(1)**

Secret Word: scary _____

Picture Clues Write Spelling
Words for each sentence.

6–7. The girl **(1)** _____ is holding an

orange **(1)** _____.

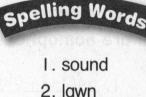

8–9. Stones from the crack **(1)** _____ in

the wall are lying on the lawn **(1)** _____.

10–12. The king, wearing his crown **(1)** _____,

cannot hear **(1)** _____ the soft

sound **(1)** _____.

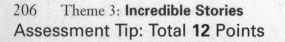

Proofreading and Writing

Proofreading Circle the five misspelled Spelling Words below. Write each word correctly.

It can be lonely (hear) in my big house. I don't hear a (werd) from morning until (darc.) This morning, however, I heard a (saft) sound. It was my friend Masha, who held out a hand for me to (skweeze.)

Spelling Words

1. clear
2. girl
3. turn
4. also
5. squeeze
6. dark
7. soft
8. north
9. her
10. new
11. here
12. our
13. knew
14. word

1. here **(1 point)**
2. word **(1)**
3. dark **(1)**
4. soft **(1)**
5. squeeze **(1)**

Which Word? Write the Spelling Word that best fits each group of words.

6. understood or ___ knew **(1)**
7. unused or ___ new **(1)**
8. in addition ___ also **(1)**
9. sunny and ___ clear **(1)**
10. his or her ___ her **(1)**
11. opposite of south ___ north **(1)**
12. boy and ___ girl **(1)**
13. to spin, circle, or ___ turn **(1)**
14. we, us, ___ our **(1)**

Write Directions On another sheet of paper, write directions telling the giant how to get from your school to your house. Use the Spelling Review Words. Responses will vary. **(6)**

Student Handbook

Contents

Spelling

How to Study a Word   **211**

Words Often Misspelled   **212**

Take-Home Word Lists   **213**

Grammar and Usage

Problem Words   **225**

Proofreading Checklist   **226**

Proofreading Marks   **227**

How to Study a Word

1. LOOK at the word.
► What does the word mean?
► What letters are in the word?
► Name and touch each letter.

2. SAY the word.
► Listen for the consonant sounds.
► Listen for the vowel sounds.

3. THINK about the word.
► How is each sound spelled?
► Close your eyes and picture the word.
► What familiar spelling patterns do you see?
► What other words have the same spelling patterns?

4. WRITE the word.
► Think about the sounds and the letters.
► Form the letters correctly.

5. CHECK the spelling.
► Did you spell the word the same way it is spelled in your word list?
► If you did not spell the word correctly, write the word again.

about	don't	I'd		
again	down	I'll		
almost		I'm	outside	tonight
a lot	enough	into		too
also	every	its	people	two
always	everybody	it's	pretty	
am				until
and	family	January	really	
another	favorite		right	very
anyone	February	knew		
anyway	field	know	said	want
around	finally		Saturday	was
	for	letter	school	Wednesday
beautiful	found	like	some	we're
because	friend	little	something	where
been	from	lose	started	while
before		lying	stopped	who
brought	getting		sure	whole
buy	girl	might	swimming	world
	goes	morning		would
cannot	going	mother	than	wouldn't
can't	guess	myself	that's	write
clothes			their	writing
coming	happily	never	them	
could	have	new	then	you
cousin	haven't	now	there	your
	heard		they	
does	her	off	thought	
didn't	here	one	through	
different	his	other	to	
done	how	our	today	

The Ballad of Mulan

More Short Vowels
/ŏ/ → lot
/ŭ/ → rub

Spelling Words
1. pond
2. luck
3. drop
4. lot
5. rub
6. does
7. drum
8. sock
9. hunt
10. crop
11. shut
12. won

Challenge Words
1. dodge
2. dusk

My Study List
Add your own spelling words on the back. →

Off to Adventure!
Reading-Writing Workshop

Look for familiar spelling patterns in these words to help you remember their spellings.

Spelling Words
1. have
2. haven't
3. found
4. around
5. one
6. than
7. then
8. them
9. before
10. because
11. other
12. mother

Challenge Words
1. family
2. cousin
3. everybody
4. guess

My Study List
Add your own spelling words on the back. →

The Lost and Found

Short Vowels
/ă/ → last
/ĕ/ → smell
/ĭ/ → mix

Spelling Words
1. mix
2. milk
3. smell
4. last
5. head
6. friend
7. class
8. left
9. thick
10. send
11. thin
12. stick

Challenge Words
1. empty
2. glance

My Study List
Add your own spelling words on the back. →

Name _____

My Study List

1. _____
2. _____
3. _____
4. _____
5. _____
6. _____
7. _____
8. _____
9. _____
10. _____

Review Words

1. test
2. dish

How to Study a Word

Look at the word.
Say the word.
Think about the word.
Write the word.
Check the spelling.

Name _____

My Study List

1. _____
2. _____
3. _____
4. _____
5. _____
6. _____
7. _____
8. _____
9. _____
10. _____

How to Study a Word

Look at the word.
Say the word.
Think about the word.
Write the word.
Check the spelling.

Name _____

My Study List

1. _____
2. _____
3. _____
4. _____
5. _____
6. _____
7. _____
8. _____
9. _____
10. _____

Review Words

1. hop
2. much

How to Study a Word

Look at the word.
Say the word.
Think about the word.
Write the word.
Check the spelling.

The Keeping Quilt

More Long Vowel Spellings

| /ā/ | → | p**ai**nt, cl**ay** |
| /ē/ | → | l**ea**ve, f**ee**l |

Spelling Words

1. paint
2. clay
3. feel
4. leave
5. neighbor
6. eight
7. seem
8. speak
9. paid
10. lay
11. need
12. weigh

Challenge Words

1. needle
2. crayon

My Study List
Add your own spelling words on the back. →

Off to Adventure!
Spelling Review

Spelling Words

1. last
2. mix
3. stick
4. lot
5. sock
6. hunt
7. wide
8. grade
9. thick
10. send
11. class
12. pond
13. luck
14. drum
15. save
16. cube
17. smile
18. left
19. smell
20. thin
21. drop
22. shut
23. huge
24. note
25. life

See the back for Challenge Words.

My Study List
Add your own spelling words on the back. →

The Waterfall

The Vowel-Consonant-*e* Pattern

/ā/	→	s**a**v**e**
/ī/	→	l**i**f**e**
/ō/	→	sm**o**k**e**
/yōō/	→	h**u**g**e**

Spelling Words

1. smoke
2. huge
3. save
4. life
5. wide
6. come
7. mine
8. grade
9. smile
10. note
11. cube
12. love

Challenge Words

1. escape
2. slope

My Study List
Add your own spelling words on the back. →

Take-Home Word List

Take-Home Word List

Take-Home Word List

Name _____

Name _____

Name _____

My Study List

1. _____
2. _____
3. _____
4. _____
5. _____
6. _____
7. _____
8. _____
9. _____
10. _____

Review Words

1. side
2. hope

My Study List

1. _____
2. _____
3. _____
4. _____
5. _____
6. _____
7. _____
8. _____
9. _____
10. _____

Challenge Words

1. glance
2. empty
3. dusk
4. slope
5. escape

My Study List

1. _____
2. _____
3. _____
4. _____
5. _____
6. _____
7. _____
8. _____
9. _____
10. _____

Review Words

1. clean
2. play

How to Study a Word

Look at the word.
Say the word.
Think about the word.
Write the word.
Check the spelling.

How to Study a Word

Look at the word.
Say the word.
Think about the word.
Write the word.
Check the spelling.

How to Study a Word

Look at the word.
Say the word.
Think about the word.
Write the word.
Check the spelling.

The Talking Cloth

Three-Letter Clusters and Unexpected Consonant Patterns

spring

street

throw

/n/ ➔ **kn**ee

/r/ ➔ **wr**ap

/ch/ ➔ wa**tch**

Spelling Words

1. spring
2. knee
3. throw
4. patch
5. strong
6. wrap
7. three
8. watch
9. street
10. know
11. spread
12. write

Challenge Words

1. strength
2. kitchen

Anthony Reynoso: Born to Rope

The Long *o* Sound

/ō/ ➔ c**oa**ch,

bl**ow**, h**o**ld

Spelling Words

1. coach
2. blow
3. float
4. hold
5. sew
6. though
7. sold
8. soap
9. row
10. own
11. both
12. most

Challenge Words

1. tomorrow
2. program

Celebrating Traditions

Reading-Writing Workshop

Look for familiar spelling patterns in these words to help you remember their spellings.

Spelling Words

1. now
2. off
3. for
4. almost
5. also
6. can't
7. cannot
8. about
9. always
10. today
11. until
12. again

Challenge Words

1. February
2. January
3. Saturday
4. Wednesday

My Study List
Add your own spelling words on the back. ➔

My Study List
Add your own spelling words on the back. ➔

My Study List
Add your own spelling words on the back. ➔

Name _____

My Study List

1. _____
2. _____
3. _____
4. _____
5. _____
6. _____
7. _____
8. _____
9. _____
10. _____

How to Study a Word

Look at the word.
Say the word.
Think about the word.
Write the word.
Check the spelling.

Name _____

My Study List

1. _____
2. _____
3. _____
4. _____
5. _____
6. _____
7. _____
8. _____
9. _____
10. _____

Review Words

1. cold
2. slow

How to Study a Word

Look at the word.
Say the word.
Think about the word.
Write the word.
Check the spelling.

Name _____

My Study List

1. _____
2. _____
3. _____
4. _____
5. _____
6. _____
7. _____
8. _____
9. _____
10. _____

Review Words

1. catch
2. two

How to Study a Word

Look at the word.
Say the word.
Think about the word.
Write the word.
Check the spelling.

Dogzilla

The Vowel Sounds in *clown* and *lawn*

/ou/ ➤ cl**ow**n, s**ou**nd

/ô/ ➤ l**aw**n, cl**o**th, t**a**lk

Spelling Words

1. clown
2. lawn
3. talk
4. sound
5. cloth
6. would
7. also
8. mouth
9. crown
10. soft
11. count
12. law

Challenge Words

1. bounce
2. officer

My Study List
Add your own spelling words on the back. ➤

Celebrating Traditions
Spelling Review

Spelling Words

1. speak
2. feel
3. seem
4. most
5. both
6. know
7. street
8. lie
9. need
10. paint
11. hold
12. float
13. three
14. spread
15. mind
16. might
17. lay
18. leave
19. own
20. row
21. wrap
22. patch
23. tie
24. wild
25. bright

See the back for Challenge Words.

My Study List
Add your own spelling words on the back. ➤

Dancing Rainbows

The Long *i* Sound

/ī/ ➤ br**igh**t, w**i**ld, d**ie**

Spelling Words

1. wild
2. bright
3. die
4. sight
5. child
6. pie
7. fight
8. lie
9. tight
10. tie
11. might
12. mind

Challenge Words

1. design
2. delight

My Study List
Add your own spelling words on the back. ➤

Take-Home Word List

Name _____

My Study List

1. _____
2. _____
3. _____
4. _____
5. _____
6. _____
7. _____
8. _____
9. _____
10. _____

Review Words

1. find
2. high

How to Study a Word

Look at the word.
Say the word.
Think about the word.
Write the word.
Check the spelling.

220

Take-Home Word List

Name _____

My Study List

1. _____
2. _____
3. _____
4. _____
5. _____
6. _____
7. _____
8. _____
9. _____
10. _____

Challenge Words

1. needle
2. tomorrow
3. program
4. kitchen
5. design

How to Study a Word

Look at the word.
Say the word.
Think about the word.
Write the word.
Check the spelling.

220

Take-Home Word List

Name _____

My Study List

1. _____
2. _____
3. _____
4. _____
5. _____
6. _____
7. _____
8. _____
9. _____
10. _____

Review Words

1. town
2. small

How to Study a Word

Look at the word.
Say the word.
Think about the word.
Write the word.
Check the spelling.

220

Raising Dragons

The /j/, /k/, and /kw/ Sounds

/j/ ➡ **j**eans, lar**ge**, **g**ym

/k/ ➡ par**k**, qui**ck**, pi**c**ni**c**

/kw/ ➡ **qu**ick

Spelling Words

1. large
2. gym
3. skin
4. quick
5. picnic
6. judge
7. park
8. jeans
9. crack
10. orange
11. second
12. squeeze

Challenge Words

1. courage
2. insect

My Study List
Add your own
spelling words
on the back. ➡

221

The Mysterious Giant of Barletta

Vowel + /r/ Sounds

/är/ ➡ d**ar**k

/î\r/ ➡ cl**ear**

/ôr/ ➡ n**or**th

/ûr/ ➡ h**er**, g**ir**l, t**ur**n, w**or**k

Spelling Words

1. girl
2. clear
3. her
4. turn
5. dark
6. work
7. smart
8. word
9. hurt
10. serve
11. north
12. third

Challenge Words

1. tornado
2. scurried

My Study List
Add your own
spelling words
on the back. ➡

221

Incredible Stories

Reading-Writing Workshop

Look for familiar spelling patterns in these words to help you remember their spellings.

Spelling Words

1. and
2. said
3. goes
4. going
5. some
6. something
7. you
8. your
9. friend
10. school
11. where
12. myself

Challenge Words

1. tonight
2. lying
3. field
4. enough

My Study List
Add your own
spelling words
on the back. ➡

221

Name _____

My Study List

1. _____
2. _____
3. _____
4. _____
5. _____
6. _____
7. _____
8. _____
9. _____
10. _____

How to Study a Word

Look at the word.
Say the word.
Think about the word.
Write the word.
Check the spelling.

Name _____

My Study List

1. _____
2. _____
3. _____
4. _____
5. _____
6. _____
7. _____
8. _____
9. _____
10. _____

Review Words

1. hard
2. morning

How to Study a Word

Look at the word.
Say the word.
Think about the word.
Write the word.
Check the spelling.

Name _____

My Study List

1. _____
2. _____
3. _____
4. _____
5. _____
6. _____
7. _____
8. _____
9. _____
10. _____

Review Words

1. rock
2. job

How to Study a Word

Look at the word.
Say the word.
Think about the word.
Write the word.
Check the spelling.

Incredible Stories
Spelling Review

Spelling Words

1. sound	14. second
2. crown	15. here
3. word	16. new
4. her	17. soft
5. crack	18. turn
6. orange	19. north
7. hear	20. skin
8. our	21. gym
9. also	22. jeans
10. girl	23. hour
11. dark	24. knew
12. clear	25. lawn
13. squeeze	

See the back for Challenge Words

My Study List
Add your own spelling words on the back. ➡

The Garden of Abdul Gasazi

Homophones
Homophones are words that sound alike but have different spellings and meanings.

Spelling Words

1. hear
2. here
3. new
4. knew
5. its
6. it's
7. our
8. hour
9. there
10. their
11. they're

Challenge Words

1. seen
2. scene

My Study List
Add your own spelling words on the back. ➡

Name _____

My Study List

1. _____
2. _____
3. _____
4. _____
5. _____
6. _____
7. _____
8. _____
9. _____
10. _____

Review Words

1. eye
2. I

How to Study a Word

Look at the word.
Say the word.
Think about the word.
Write the word.
Check the spelling.

224

Take-Home Word List

Name _____

My Study List

1. _____
2. _____
3. _____
4. _____
5. _____
6. _____
7. _____
8. _____
9. _____
10. _____

Challenge Words

1. officer
2. scurried
3. insect
4. seen
5. scene

How to Study a Word

Look at the word.
Say the word.
Think about the word.
Write the word.
Check the spelling.

224

Problem Words

Words	Rules	Examples
are our	*Are* is a verb. *Our* is a possessive pronoun.	<u>Are</u> these gloves yours? This is <u>our</u> car.
doesn't don't	Use *doesn't* with singular nouns, *he*, *she*, and *it*. Use *don't* with plural nouns, *I*, *you*, *we*, and *they*.	Dad <u>doesn't</u> swim. We <u>don't</u> swim.
good well	Use the adjective *good* to describe nouns. Use the adverb *well* to describe verbs.	The weather looks <u>good</u>. She sings <u>well</u>.
its it's	*Its* is a possessive pronoun. *It's* means "it is" (contraction).	The dog wagged <u>its</u> tail. <u>It's</u> cold today.
let leave	*Let* means "to allow." *Leave* means "to go away from" or "to let stay."	Please <u>let</u> me go swimming. I will <u>leave</u> soon. <u>Leave</u> it on my desk.
set sit	*Set* means "to put." *Sit* means "to rest or stay in one place."	<u>Set</u> the vase on the table. Please <u>sit</u> in this chair.
their there they're	*Their* means "belonging to them." *There* means "at or in that place." *They're* means "they are" (contraction).	<u>Their</u> coats are on the bed. Is Carlos <u>there</u>? <u>They're</u> going to the store.
two to too	*Two* is a number *To* means "toward." *Too* means "also" or "more than enough.	I bought <u>two</u> shirts. A cat ran <u>to</u> the tree. Can we go <u>too</u>? I ate <u>too</u> many peas.
your you're	*Your* is a possessive pronoun. *You're* means "you are" (contraction).	Are these <u>your</u> glasses? <u>You're</u> late again!

Read each question below. Then check your paper. Correct any mistakes you find. After you have corrected them, put a check mark in the box next to the question.

☐ 1. Did I indent each paragraph?

☐ 2. Does each sentence tell one complete thought?

☐ 3. Did I end each sentence with the correct end mark?

☐ 4. Did I begin each sentence with a capital letter?

☐ 5. Did I use capital letters correctly in other places?

☐ 6. Did I use commas correctly?

☐ 7. Did I spell all the words the right way?

Are there other problem areas you should watch for? Make your own proofreading checklist.

☐ _____

☐ _____

☐ _____

☐ _____

☐ _____

☐ _____

☐ _____

Mark	Explanation	Examples
¶	Begin a new paragraph. Indent the paragraph.	¶We went to an air show last Saturday. Eight jets flew across the sky in the shape of V's, X's, and diamonds.
∧	Add letters, words, or sentences.	The leaves were red ∧and orange.
℘	Take out words, sentences, and punctuation marks. Correct spelling.	The sky is bright ~~blew~~ blue. Huge clouds, move quickly.
/	Change a capital letter to a small letter.	The Fireflies blinked in the dark.
≡	Change a small letter to a capital letter.	New York city is exciting.